We, The Aborigines

DOUGLAS LOCKWOOD

 J.B. BOOKS AUSTRALIA

Other books by Douglas Lockwood:

CROCODILES AND OTHER PEOPLE

FAIR DINKUM

LIFE ON THE DALY RIVER
 (with Nancy Polishuk)

I, THE ABORIGINAL

This edition is an exclusive production published in 1998 for
J.B. Books Pty Ltd
PO Box 118
Marleston 5033
South Australia
Phone/Fax (08) 8297 1669

First published in Australia in hardcover 1963
by Cassell Australia Ltd
Walkabout Pocketbook edition first published in
the British Commonwealth 1970 by Ure Smith, Sydney

Printed in Australia by McPherson's Printing Group

National Library of Australia Cataloguing-in-Publication data
Lockwood, Douglas, 1918-1980
  We, the Aborigines.

 ISBN 1 86302 622 3
 1. Aborigines, Australian. I. Title.
 305.89915

This book is dedicated
to the memory of
BILL HARNEY
He was the only white
man I knew who could
think like an aboriginal.
They were his friends.
He was their friend.

Author's Note

I have tried in this book to show the Australian Aborigines as human beings rather than scientific phenomena, as people rather than things. I have attempted to tell at least one facet of their lives in each story in the hope that, taken as a whole, a fairly comprehensive picture will emerge.

I talked personally with most of the men and women whose photographs are reproduced. But where direct speech is attributed to any of them, it is mine and not theirs.

The word 'blackfeller' is not used is any derogatory sense. They use it constantly themselves.

DOUGLAS LOCKWOOD

Contents

Some of the poems by Bill Harney in his *Tales from the Aborigines* are reprinted by kind permission of the publishers, Robert Hale Limited.

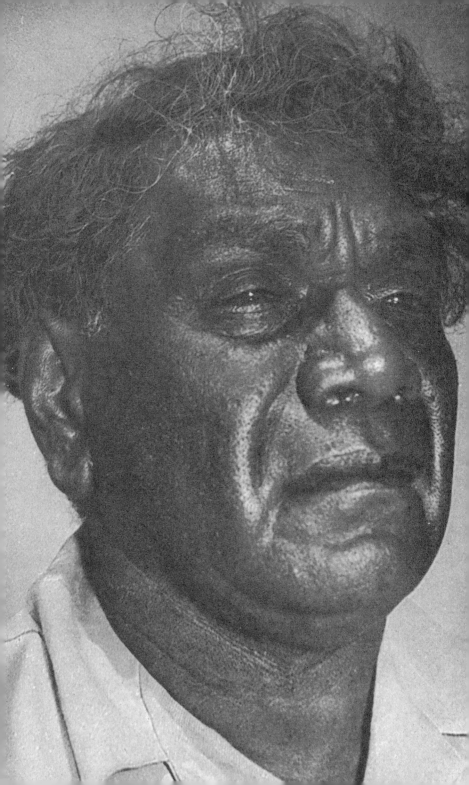

Albert Namatjira

ARANDA TRIBE

CENTRAL AUSTRALIA

←———————————————————————

HE WAS THE MOST FAMOUS aboriginal of them all, a man who did more to win respect for his tribespeople than any other. Now he is dead. His bones lie in a white man's cemetery at Alice Springs, a desegregated corpse accepted in death by men who shunned and often reviled him in life.

His signature is on paintings which hang in art galleries and embassies and private homes all over the world. He was paid as much as £200 for a single picture. In one year he made £7000, and spent it all on his friends. He was Aranda Bank Unlimited.

Sharing with his people was a tribal obligation learned at his initiation as a man. But the undeniable tribal law was to lead him to grief and tragedy. As a citizen, Namatjira could drink alcohol. The white man's law said he must not share it with his relatives who were not citizens. The black man's law said that he must; it won and Namatjira lost.

One night near his camp at Morris Soak a tribal woman was murdered by her husband in a fit of rage after he had drunk liquor Albert supplied. He was never the same again. I will always remember him entering the Coroner's Court at Alice Springs. He walked slowly and shakily. He bowed solemnly, grief in every line of his face.

His long grey hair was curly and untidy, just like an artist's. He was thin and ill and distressed. He looked older than his years, and haggard. His face was grim, with never the trace of a smile.

The tragedy of all the Australian aborigines was written in his eyes — forlorn, incredibly sad eyes that would have been weeping if set in a white face.

But an aboriginal man doesn't cry, especially if he has the stature of an Aranda and the name of a Namatjira. Even if his heart is crying.

He was the descendant of pagans, and yet took an oath on a Christian Bible.

'It is the truth,' he said, and gave his evidence: 'I went to sleep . . . my head wasn't right . . . I was full . . . I didn't know about the murder until I woke up next morning . . .'

The witness signed his depositions with the signature that hangs on walls in hundreds of homes at the bottom right-hand corner of pleasant watercolours. Then he stumbled from the room, a broken man. And soon he was dead. My friend Bill Harney wrote his epitaph:

> Sleep on, Ungata, sleep. The spirits of your tribe
> Weep by Kulrungga's steep and stony peak;
> The Finke's white gums and ti-trees sigh and sway
> As church-bells toll to bless the weak and meek.
>
> The weak and meek . . . 'twas you who blazed the trail,
> A giant midst the ashes of your land;
> Painting a dream where ritual song-men died
> As tribal waters choked with drifting sand.
>
> 'Twas you who showed us all the land you loved,
> Loved above critics' learned jibe and scorn;
> Amidst the dust your colours ever flowed,
> The hues of evening and the golden morn.
>
> The domes of Katatjuta and the blue
> Of early dawn by Sonder's sacred peak:
> The red of Karinyarri and the white
> Ghost-gums that gleam beside the sandy creek.

You shared with us the pleasure of your art,
And freely gave your kin the wealth you earned;
Deep in the ashes of your clan you toiled,
Painting by firelight as the mulgas burned.

Sleep well, my friend . . . the spirits of your tribe
Grieve on with those who understood your worth;
The bellbird calls at dawn to tell your clan
That peace is yours at last . . . O! Mother-earth!

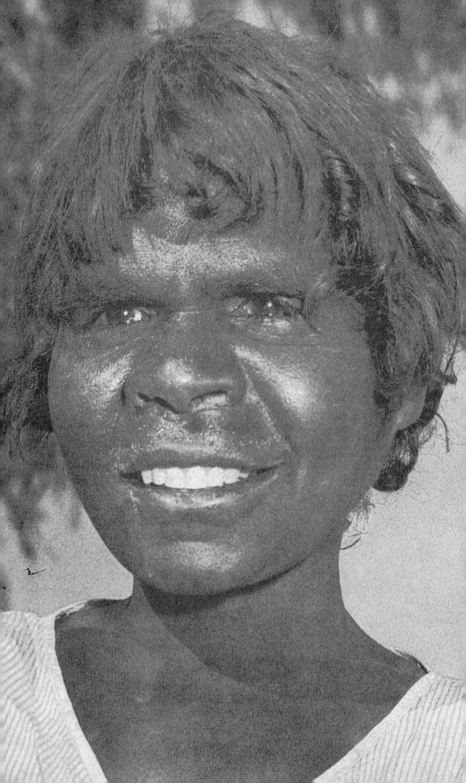

Topsy

DJUMINDJUNG TRIBE

NORTH AUSTRALIA

←————————————————————————————————

I AM A SYMBOL OF times past, the daughter of a survivor of white man's inhumanity to black man in the days when this country was being taken from us. The white man's word for that is Settlement.

Usurpation of tribal land has always been accompanied by great cruelties and immense suffering for the dispossessed, whether they are white, black or brindle. The history of colonial empires gives ample and terrible proof of that.

It wasn't long after Captain Cook landed on the east coast in the eighteenth century that the tribulations of the tribes began.

Our women were caught and raped. Our men were murdered if they showed the slightest disposition to resist. We could have forgotten the rape and borne the murders if it hadn't been that simultaneously we were chased away from our lands as though we, and not the white men, were the interlopers.

Nor was that the only punishment of dispossession. Anyone who understands the aborigines knows they are tied to tribal land like fish to water, like birds to the air. Deprive them of their natural environment and they soon die. But to take our tribal land from us meant even more; for it is indissolubly linked with our religion. That's where our totems are, our Dreamings, our ritual places, the spirits from whom our reincarnation springs. To be deprived of the land was bad enough. To be deprived simultaneously of the basis of all our beliefs, the wells from which our

17

traditions and corroborees flowed — this was double-dyed murder because it meant destruction of the will to live.

Is it to be wondered at, therefore, that the tribes soon ceased to resist and were decimated. Is it surprising that their morale and their morality deteriorated to the extent that they ceased to care — and became human blowflies on the scrap heaps of civilisation.

If you doubt me, then let me tell you My Mother's Story — the story she told me when I was a small child of one incident which shows how the land was settled and my people tamed. I have remembered it all my life:

'Mother-belong-me (that is, my own grandmother) bin die . . . poor feller . . . when I was little-bit kid . . . die from guts-ache after eating big feed of rice given we by the cattle station boss. . . .

'We bin come into that station proper hungry. Nobody savvy white man's horse is sacred to him and danger to kill. Well, we bin kill and eat fat-feller horse and everybody happy.

'Now that white-feller Boss was called by blackfeller "Paddy-with-shortfeller-leg." He was a properly-no-good-bugger. When he find out that we bin kill'em good horse he get proper cross. Straightaway he bin cook big feed of rice with plenty sugar, make'im-sweet-feller, but that cunning bugger also sing-it with arsenic poison. Nobody savvy that until later . . . after we eat'im.

'Now when all-about eat and start get guts-ache Uncle-belong-me savvy that rice got poison. So he make we-all dive into waterhole and eat stinkin-mud from bottom so that we spew everywhere. But no matter spew, some people bin die with big pain and we bin cry-out no-more-little-bit for dead-one . . . Mumma-belong-me . . . poor feller . . . she die first-time.

'But before she die she bin poke mud longa my throat and guts to make me spew. It was proper no-good business I tell you. Some people no-more die but roll on ground and cry-out properly loud-feller, all-a-time grabbin' guts.

'As we cry out that Paddy-with-shortfeller-leg and blackfeller from another tribe come down with rifles and fire shots into we. No-matter got guts-ache, we all bin get up and run for long cane grass that grows longa creek. There we lie all-a-same wild bullock that try to dodge mustering.

'I bin dead-fright when I hear rifle-shots in grass near-to . . . but they no-more bin find me. Might-be they shoot some people while they lie there . . . I dunno for I no-more savvy how many die from guts-ache and I bin only little-feller girl.

'All-about very glad when sun go down and we hear Paddy-with-short-feller-leg go away to him house. When dark come we sneak out like wallabies and footrace no-more-little-bit for hill country. Sometime I bin knock up longa wind and legs. I can't walk so my Uncle carry me longa shoulder while he run . . . and he run . . . and he run . . . until he fall-down. But that Paddy-with-shortfeller-leg can't leave we alone. Tomor-row, sun-up, he gets horses and chase we into big hill country. We climb until horse can't go there . . . then we find caves and sit-down . . . proper hungry . . . proper thirsty. . . .

'Two . . . three . . . day we sit there with no-more tucker . . . till Uncle-belong-me say he go down for kangaroo. From where we sit we can see him walkin' . . . dodgin'-about be'ind bushes. Then we hear rifle shot and his hands bin throw up in air . . . he fall down, dead-finish.

'We still hungry so that night grandfather-belong-me went down in the dark. He bin come back with plenty meat that we cook on open fires until all-about got properly swell-up bingy.

'I wonder why all-about people don't want to eat first-time . . . and when they eat I wonder why they look so sad, 'cos it taste good. But now me old woman and I savvy they get meat from body of Uncle-belong-me. I get proper mad at whitefeller who made we do this terrible thing.'

That was the story my Mother told me. I have never forgotten it. I never will. I have lived with whitefellers in my time. Some are good and kind. Some are just plain rubbish. But none of them could be as bad as that Paddy-with-shortfeller-leg who made my people into cannibals.

Jack Kelly

ARANDA TRIBE

CENTRAL AUSTRALIA

◀━━━━━━━━━━━━━━━━━━━━━━━━━━━━━━━━━━━━━━━

I KNOW EXACTLY WHAT YOU'RE going to say.

'What a wonderful white beard!'

It's all right, as long as I don't set fire to it again.

That happened once when I was lighting my pipe with a firestick.

I was clean-shaven in a flash. My skin lifted, too.

Now I have fitted my pipe with an extra-long stem. I daren't smoke cigarettes. I should really stick to chewing. Every time I light up I'm afraid.

Let me introduce myself: I'm Jack Kelly of the Aranda tribe at Alice Springs, Central Australia.

Being something of a personality, I was invited to fly to Canberra to meet the Queen Mother.

Actually, SHE asked to meet ME. I suppose she had heard about me from the Prime Minister or someone like that.

After all, I hold Cabinet rank. I'm an Elder of the Arandas.

I thought the Queen Mother was a nice lady. I offered her a plug of my chewing tobacco but she said she didn't use it.

On the way to Canberra I couldn't understand why the wings of the aeroplane didn't flap.

Every other bird I've seen flaps its wings.

But not the Vickers Viscount — well, only a weeny bit when we flew through rough weather.

When I was a young man I walked from Alice Springs to Oodnadatta through the lands of the Loritjas and the Pitjentjarras.

We were on the track for one month.

I flew from Alice Springs to Oodnadatta in less than two hours, and I could see the lands of the Arandas, the Loritjas, the Pitjentjarras and the Wailbris all at once.

Now my friends back at Amoonguna settlement call me Jack the Liar. Two hours to Oodnadatta indeed!

I told them about the oceans which none of my friends have seen.

They laughed and called me Liar.

I told them about Sydney Harbour Bridge with trains and buses and cars — hundreds of them — all running across it at the same time.

The only bridge they've seen is the footbridge across the Todd River at Alice Springs.

'Tell us about the bridge again, Jack,' they ask. Then they laugh and call me Liar.

I haven't even got a wife who, if only because of her loyalty, would have to believe me.

No, she's not dead. I'm single. I've never had a wife. I'm the only man of my age in the tribe who hasn't been married.

Sometimes it has been cold and lonely on the ground at night with no old woman to keep the fire stoked, to bring me food and a light for my pipe.

But it won't be long now. I'm tired and disillusioned and soon I will die.

I'll be glad, too, for then I won't be able to hear that mocking laughter.

I was a small boy when the first white men came to this country. They were German preachers who went out to Hermannsburg with their goats and cattle and began a mission which is there today. Not all of us believed the stories they told of a god who lives in the sky . . .

> The God-men say, 'When die go sky
> Through pearly gates where rivers flow'.
> The God-men say, 'When die we fly
> Just like eagle-hawk and crow'.
> Might be . . . might be . . . I don't know.

But they also told us about the big trains and the cities and the tall buildings, and when I went there I found they had told the truth.

So now I wonder if it is also true that there are pearly gates and rivers in the sky, and that I'll fly like an eagle-hawk when I die.

It wasn't long before I was born that the biggest miracle of all time came to the aborigines. It remains so today, in spite of the Sydney Harbour Bridge.

My father told me of the day when white men arrived with horses and waggons loaded with poles and wire.

'Ah,' my people said, 'they're going to build a big fence.'

It was a big fence, all right. The poles were thirty feet high. There was only one wire — and later two — on top. Obviously it wasn't meant as a paddock for cattle. In any case, the fence kept going in a straight line. And then, one day, the wires began to sing.

We were told it was a telegraph line, but we didn't know what that meant.

'Writing along sky,' they said. 'Also talk along sky. The telephone.'

A man showed my father a telephone set and said it could be used for talking to invisible men. My father wouldn't believe him. So he put the receiver to his ear and a man's voice said, 'Gooday, Jack!' My old man dropped it and ran away. He thought a spirit had spoken to him. Ninety years later, there still aren't many aborigines who like speaking on a telephone. They can't forget that it might be a devil at the other end.

Denise

WAILBRI TRIBE

CENTRAL AUSTRALIA

◄─────────────────────────────────

IT'S ALL VERY WELL FOR you to laugh. You don't have to stand up in your birthday suit and suffer the indignity of being washed in public.

Is that a nice thing for a little girl, especially with a photographer pointing his camera at her?

They say water is wonderful. I say babies can do without it.

There was a time when my people, the Wailbri, didn't have enough water to waste on washing. Every drop we could find was used for drinking and even then we were often thirsty.

I say, Give me those good old days.

Since the government came sticky-beaking in our tribal lands in the desert the children have been getting a rough time.

We have to be bathed every day. Whoever heard of such nonsense! Not only washed in water, but with soap, too. Get's in a girl's eyes — and it tastes awful.

My elder brothers and sisters fed on my mother's breast until they walked and grew teeth. Some of them weren't weaned until they were two or three years old. Then they ate goanna tail and snake.

But what happens now? Tinned baby food, government issue, for me. Ugh! And porridge. Ugh! Ugh! Looks like cement and tastes like it, too.

Nor do the indignities cease there. We have to sit at a table, if you please, and eat off plates with spoons and forks. What was wrong with a piece of lizard held in the fingers while we sat in the sand? Sure, it got a bit gritty at times — but it was all clean dirt.

Every so often I have to be examined by the nurse. She looks at my tongue and my teeth and prods me as though she has never seen one of my kind before.

If I get a cold she gives me breathing medicine for my nose. If I've got a sore chest she gives me rubbing medicine. For a bellyache I am given drinking medicine.

I tell you straight, things around here are going from bad to worse. And do you know what else they've got in store for me? School!

They're just sweating on the day when I'll be old enough to pack off with a cut lunch and a bag on my back to sit in a room learning how to read and write.

Not long ago aboriginal kids could play in the bush all day until they grew up and were ready for marriage.

Even then they didn't work: the men hunted food and the women produced babies. That's all there was to it.

But now I've got to be washed and dressed, my hair combed, my nose clean, a handkerchief tied to my dress while I learn c-a-t cat. Who cares?

Life is not what it used to be. And this, of course, is the end: to stand on a piece of old iron while your Mum gets rid of all that wonderful dirt with soap and water.

She takes no notice of my sobs. Her attitude, in fact, is 'She likes to cry otherwise she wouldn't do it. So why stop her?'

I wouldn't mind nearly as much if my mother would be like the women of the Mara tribe south of the Roper River who use the leaves of the Soap Tree. When these are rubbed in water they produce a lather. Screen stars probably would not write testimonials for it, but at least it doesn't sting the eyes and we have fun gathering the leaves.

Perhaps it does smell a little like disinfectant, as my big sister's boyfriend complains, but surely that is one of its uses?

Some people are surprised when they hear that we have a Soap Tree. But doesn't toilet soap come from the oil of coconuts, which grow on palm trees?

In fact, soap isn't the only thing we find growing on trees in the

Australian bush. Out in the desert there is a giant yam called Yallah which stores water. So does the succulent parakelia.

Trees also yield beads with which our women adorn themselves, spiked branches to make combs, witchetty grubs for food, pituri to smoke, wild honey we call Sugarbag, and fig leaves for those who can't afford a lap-lap.

Trees have other unexpected uses, too. Hollowed trunks have been used by tribal murderers to secrete corpses. And particular trees are used by black Romeos as their equivalent of Under-the-Clocks and the Eros statue.

I almost forgot another grudge. They have named me Denise. Now what do you think of THAT for an aboriginal girl's name? I might have been Nambidjimba or Nangala or Nagamara or Nabungadi or Naburula. Decent native names which everyone knows and can understand. But no! They must inflict a white-feller name upon me.

Denise, indeed!

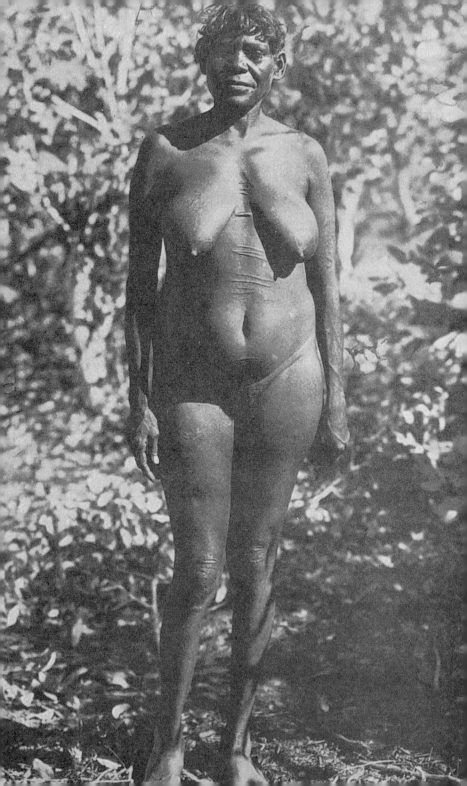

Titkerri

PITJENTJARRA TRIBE

CENTRAL AUSTRALIA

←——

> *Loveliness needs not the foreign aid of adornment,*
> *But is when unadorned adorned the most.*

I AM NOT in the least ashamed of my nakedness. If you are ashamed to look at me I suggest you turn the page; better still, turn over a new leaf by ceasing to regard the female body as pornographic or a subject for sniggering.

My name is Titkerri. I am a woman of the Pitjentjarra tribe at Areyonga, the Place of the Singing Hills, in Central Australia. I am unquestionably beautiful by all aboriginal standards.

An aboriginal man is said to be handsome if he is of medium height, has slight thighs and fine legs with well-developed calves, and is hairy only in those places where hair is natural — on the head, face, pubes and arm-pits.

A woman is beautiful when she is like me: Full pendulous breasts; a firm rounded abdomen, strong thighs, large soft eyes with long lashes, a small nose with broad nostrils, a firm chin and full lips.

I must say, however, that there is not much incentive for a tribes-woman to improve upon or even retain what beauty she has.

If we had to get into the ring and fight for our husbands like white women we might preen ourselves a little more than we do.

But what's the use? Since the day I was born, and even before that, I was promised in marriage to a hairy, smelly old man who, by the time I was old enough, was blind and senile.

Of course, I had to go with him. To have refused would have involved me in dire consequences, perhaps death. This is a kind of tribal super-annuation scheme: the old men have young wives to care for them in their dotage; to provide food, water and tobacco, if necessary, by selling their bodies to the virile young men who have been denied wives because the ancients have them all.

It sounds crazy and it is.

When the Old Man dies — and we are probably better qualified than any other women in the world to call our husbands 'Old Man' — we go to his heir just as though we were a block of land or a bank account. The heir might be a brother or a cousin who is not much younger. By the time he dies and we are able to take a young man of our own choice we are probably old and haggard ourselves. Not that the young men mind that, of course. Having been deprived for most of their lives they are only too pleased to have any aged cast-off wife. And, as they say, all women are black at night.

Perhaps this explains why we don't paint our bodies or deck ourselves in attractive, enticing finery. Our lives are governed for us long before we reach puberty. There is no need for us to come out scratching in war paint, breast plates, and armoured corselets.

One wonders how many white women would pass as beautiful if they had to be judged without their artificial aids?

In such circumstances I wouldn't be surprised if there were a greater percentage of classically beautiful women among the black people.

Imagine, for instance, how the eyes of white men would suddenly find interests elsewhere if uplift brassieres, mascara, rouge and diadems had never been invented.

Having acquired his wife easily, an aboriginal man can just as easily dispose of her. One of the compensations of tribal marriage from the male point of view is that he can divorce his wife with even greater ease than

30

the Moslem who says three times, 'I divorce thee.' An aboriginal need only say, 'Go!'

The divorce is absolute the moment she leaves.

'Women, unfortunately, do not have the same right to divorce their husbands, except in rare cases where it is proved that the man is an incurable adulterer.

There are not many divorces among tribespeople, but adultery is the prime cause of those that do occur, not because adultery in itself is regarded as such a terrible sin but because it is the result of incompatability. A man will leave a woman who strays from his swag. He will not leave one who is ugly, barren, ill-tempered, unclean, a poor cook, or shrewish.

Board of Directors

LORITJA TRIBE

CENTRAL AUSTRALIA

←——————————————————————————————————

THE WEEKLY MEETING OF OUR Board of Directors is rather informal.

We have no mahogany table or chairs, no panelled room hung with the portraits of past chairmen, no port, no cigars, and not much talk about bonus issues, price-earnings ratio, or Bank Rate.

As we squat in the dirt around a campfire, almost entirely naked, there is little chance that we could be confused with the morning-trousered Court of the Bank of England.

Those gentlemen really look after themselves. They even print their own money. Now that is something we might think about out here.

For fifteen thousand years our people have disregarded the importance of this commodity. I think it's about time we woke up to the fact that it has its uses.

Only the other day I was discussing the day's hunt with one of the young men in the tribe. I then asked him his opinion of money.

'What's that?' he asked.

'You buy things with it,' I said.

'Will it buy a wife?' he asked.

'No.'

'Will it help me hunt kangaroos?'

'No.'

'Can you eat it or drink it?'

'No.'

'Does it keep you warm at night?'

'No.'

'Then what's the use of it,' he said. 'I can get goannas and snakes, kangaroos and rats, yams and wild honey, water and a wife without it. What would I do with money?'

This is regrettably the attitude of too many of our young men. They have to be educated to the fact that money buys boomerangs and butter.

I'm told that white men love it, and especially white women. I know that it plays a significant part in the arrangement of marriage partners among them. Men have been known to cure their penury, and women their broken hearts, by acquiring it in this way.

Yet, until recent times, we didn't even know it existed. Out here in the desert there are still plenty of people who, if offered a choice between a five-pound note and a stick of tobacco, would unhesitatingly take the tobacco — something of tangible value that could be used at once.

I would be highly indignant if a man offered me fifty pounds cash for one of my wives. But I would gladly accept fifty pounds weight of flour, tea and sugar, which someone told me would be worth only about twenty-five pounds in money. That doesn't make sense to me.

Here's another thing we find difficult to understand: the government gives us food, water, clothes and houses, which cost money. But when one of my friends asked for money he was told the government didn't give that away.

There are other respects in which our idea of money seems to be irreconcilable with the white man's. The other day I hired a taxi to go from Alice Springs to Amoonguna aboriginal settlement. I had a mate out there who owed me one pound and I wanted to collect it. Next day The Boss berated me because the taxi ride cost one pound.

'You spent a pound to collect a pound. That's stupid!' he said.

I don't think so. A debt was settled, and that's different.

In our own sphere, the Council of Elders you see here has as much authority as the Conclave of Cardinals in the Catholic Church and the Central Committee of the Communist Party.

We give the tribal orders. It is on our instructions that the Kadaitcha Man and the Mulunguwa — the dreaded secret executioners — put on their symbolic black hoods and move stealthily against men who have broken the tribal commandments. Nor are we ever troubled by the same introspection as the poet who wrote:

We slew the slayer and I wonder
Who now has the debt to pay.

It is quite true that we have ordered Kadaitchas and Mulunguwas to kill. If you like, they were Hangmen's Hangmen. But surely we are absolved when it is realised that in all cases we act completely without malice. For everyone knows that a murder charge cannot be sustained unless there is 'malice aforethought.'

As Elders, we are nothing more than Defenders of the Faith, Keepers of the Dreamings, Custodians of the Culture who insist that our totems should not be desecrated nor tribesmen commit sacrilege by defiling any part of our religious observance.

If any of us fails in this task it will not be long before we are without a seat in the boardroom, uncomfortable as it is. In fact, it is quite probable that we would become the target for a Kadaitcha appointed in our absence. A vacancy would thus occur on the Board of Directors, through ejection of spear rather than effluxion of time.

By the way, Mister Chairman, I think it's time we had a few renovations done to this board-room. I can't stop scratching myself.

Jackson

ARANDA TRIBE

CENTRAL AUSTRALIA

←——————————————————————————————

THE MAN SAID, 'NIGGER, YOU take this bucket and fill'im with that yeller-feller rock you bin show me. For what you bring me I give you level-feller in flour.'

That was a long time ago, when I was a young man. I had a family to feed and the arrangement suited me well. So I went out into the hills at Arltunga where I climbed down a big hole and chipped away at the rockface with a pick.

At sun-down I had a bucketful, each piece showing veins of the yeller-feller rock that The Boss wanted so badly. I gave it to him and he seemed pleased. He went into the storeroom and came back with the bucket of flour. We made three big dampers and allabout got full-up-bingy.

The next day and the day after that for many months I filled the bucket with rocks and he filled it with flour. That was a good time. We all ate well. Sometimes when the rock was heavily streaked with yellow The Boss gave me beef as well, and occasionally sugar and tea.

At first I thought he must want to build a house with the stone but one day he took it all away to Alice Springs. When he came back I heard him muttering about 'eighty ounces to the ton,' but it made no sense to me.

Now I know that I gave him rich nuggets of gold, perhaps a hundred pounds worth in every bucketful.

But am I unhappy? No, sir. You can't eat gold. If I was offered a bucket of gold now or a bucket of flour I would unhesitatingly take the flour.

There were other minerals about which we were not nearly so diffident. They were red ochre, yellow ochre and white clay. All were used in our ceremonials to paint our bodies and our implements. They were used for rock paintings, for cave paintings, and for painting on bark.

Red ochre came from the ironstone hills around Maryvale station. At Rumbalara, not far from Finke River, we had an enormous storehouse of yellow ochre and white clay in the flat-top residuals which had been there waiting for us since the earth was made.

We are asked why it is that corroboree grounds have been placed in inaccessible areas. The chief reason is that we had to go to the ochre deposits wherever they were located. Once there, it was easier to hold our ceremonies on the spot than to carry big quantities of the minerals back to our camps, although that was sometimes done.

During the war I mined tungsten on the same contract basis as I had mined gold: a bucket of black wolfram ore for a bucket of rations.

It was needed in big quantities for hardening steel — in such big quantities, in fact, that I had to employ sub-contractors to help me. I paid them half a bucket of flour for a bucket of ore. My employees seemed quite pleased with the arrangement. After all, half a bucket of flour is better than no damper. However, there were times during this period when I was accused of exploiting them. Certainly I had cornered the market. And certainly I was getting flour without working. But there must be a middleman in every undertaking.

These days when I'm asked my occupation I say, 'Retired miner.'

I had to retire because my eyes are not quite what they seem. I'm told that they are wide open and appear to see.

Yet I am blind.

The dreaded trachoma and dust from the mines has drawn filmy shutters over the irises and pupils. I can barely distinguish between night and day.

Ah! What happened to the sun just then? A flash-bulb, you say? It was like the sun bursting in my face.

My name is Jackson of the Aranda tribe. I live at Amoonguna settlement near Alice Springs with a few old mates who have also been contract miners.

Three of us share an aluminium hut. We make our campfire in the centre of the concrete floor. There is no chimney and the smoke hazard inside is generally very bad but we are all used to it.

Mr. Government brings our rations every day — meat, bread, tea, sugar and tobacco.

And I have never yet been asked to contribute a bucketful of stone for any of it. I think this man Government must be rich.

I know he gets plenty of money from the black men who go to Court for 'abo drink liquor.'

But white-feller way is funny sometimes. One day I went before the Big-Feller Judge because I drank some grog.

'Jackson, you must pay one pound to Government because you drink,' he said.

I told him I didn't have any money.

'All right,' he said, 'Government will pay for you.'

Perhaps it's because I'm blind that I can't see the sense in this. Or perhaps it's because I'm just a dumb old blackfeller.

I dunno.

Old Barney

NANGOMERI TRIBE

DALY RIVER DISTRICT, N.T.

←───────────────────────────────────

AND JESUS SAITH UNTO THEM, Children have ye any meat? They answered him, No.

And he said unto them, Cast the net on the right side of the ship and ye shall find. They cast therefore, and now they were not able to draw it for the multitude of fishes.

That's how it is with me sometimes, here on the Daly River. I get sick and tired of the taste and smell of fish.

Mind you, I haven't any Biblical nets becoming miraculously jammed with barramundi. I catch every one the hard way, with a three-pronged spear.

But there is never any shortage because the river teems with barramundi, mullet, trevally and snapper.

Also sharks and crocodiles which are both very fond of humanity, especially raw. They've swallowed a few black Jonahs who have never been regurgitated.

The Disciples who gathered with Jesus at the Sea of Tiberias so very long ago would not have been worried by famine had they lived here with us.

I'm an old man now. My name is Barney Barrgirr of the Nangomeri tribe. I have been on the Daly River all my life. Yet never once have I known a black man in this district to be hungry. Old Man River provides. I paddle along in my dugout canoe, spear poised, waiting for a big fish to come near.

When then happens . . . Whish! and I've got him. Always.

Therefore I find it exceedingly difficult to understand the blind stupidity of some of my people.

White men have tortured themselves since the beginning of time by scratching miserable livings in the world's most inhospitable deserts.

It is the same with the aborigines. We are supposed to be the descendants of the Dravidians who migrated to Australia about 15,000 years ago from India and Ceylon. Perhaps they came in bark canoes. Perhaps they floated across the ocean on logs, driven by the tide and the currents. Or they may have come over the land bridge which was once said to exist.

What I cannot understand is why some of them left the seas and rivers on the north coast where they landed and migrated to the sandy deserts in the interior where they had to hunt constantly to find enough rats and mice and water to stay alive.

It is as though they were cast out from The Chosen by some pagan god and banished like the Children of Israel by a wicked Pharaoh.

Now they belong to another race. The Arandas, the Pitjentjarras, the Loritjas, the Wailbris, the Anmatjiras and the Kaiditj of Central Australia are totally dissimilar from the coastal and river people like myself — the Nangomeri, the Malak Malak, the Wargite, the Tiwi, the Andilyaugwa, the Anula.

They are dirty, dishevelled, demoralized, thirsty and hungry.

We are clean people. We wash every day. But those Centralians! Eating rats and snakes and living eternally in their own filth. They should be ashamed.

They're not brothers of ours.

Ethnically, I admit, we're from the same stock.

At least we all have black skins.

But otherwise we resemble them as much as a desert Bedouin resembles an Eskimo.

It's not often I sound off like this about other people, but to a Saltwater Man dirt is abhorrent.

THE HUNTER'S CYCLE

This morning a storm-bird was calling. Quoth he,
'I have come from those countries far over the sea
'To put silver blooms on the cherry-plum tree.'

The plum trees replied 'And our blooms bring the rain
'That floods o'er the rice-swamps, that ripens the grain
'Where magpie-geese nest on the red-lily plain.'

In whispering cold winds the bottle-brush tree
Swayed as it sang its song that the bee
Go gather its nectar for you, and for me.

The wattle is flowering, and down by the stream,
The hunters are fishing the fat silver bream,
Their campfires by ti-trees are ever agleam.

The cycle of nature goes sweeping around,
The red-coral blooms tell of yams that abound
In jungles where berries and fig-trees are found.

By these the wise hunter is ever foretold,
Through bird, tree and flower how seasons unfold,
The Wet and the Dry, the Hot and the Cold.

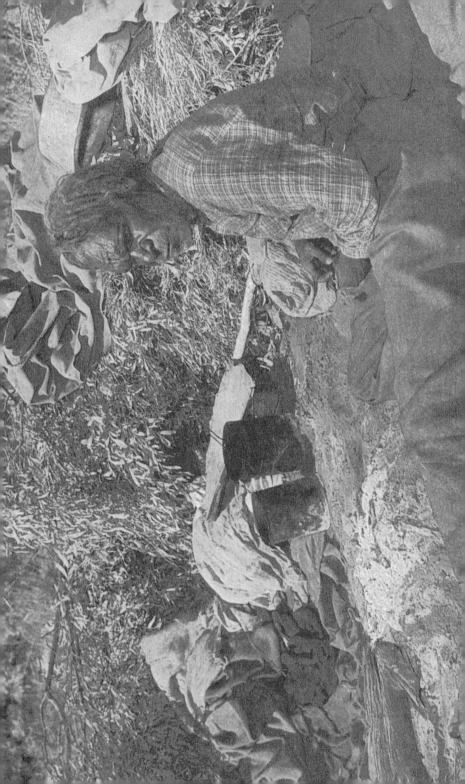

Jack Jungula . . .

WAILBRI TRIBE

YUENDUMU, CENTRAL AUSTRALIA

◀————————————————————————————

A SOFT ANSWER TURNETH AWAY wrath but grievous words stir up anger. The tongue of the wise useth knowledge aright but the mouths of fools poureth out foolishness. All the ways of man are clean in his own eyes but the Lord weigheth the spirits.

Solomon said so.

I wouldn't take too much notice of Old Barney, who walks in the path of self-righteousness.

Sure, his body is clean.

But what of his heart and mind?

He has a river in which to fish, and to wash the dirt from his body.

My name is Jack Jungula of the Wailbri tribe he has disclaimed. I live at Yuendumu in the Central Australian desert.

There is no river anywhere near us. In all my life I have never seen more water at one time than I could put in those two billycans.

When rain falls it soaks straight into the parched red earth. Our natural desert seeps yield as little as one gallon of water in twenty-four hours.

And yet there are fools like Barney the Nangomeri who say that we are dirty.

Certainly we are unclean. But surely he must know that it is because we have never had enough water to use for washing.

We have often not had enough to drink. The billies are empty now — and I am thirsty. When my old woman comes I must tell her to fill them, for I am too old to walk.

45

I have lived for seventy years, every day of it in the desert. Yes, I have eaten rats and mice and snakes and much worse things than that in the long droughts.

I have never known any other home than a nomad's camp like the one you see here: a windbreak of mulga bushes, a few blankets given to us by the white men, two billies, and a fire.

We might stay in a camp like this for days or weeks or months, depending on food and water.

My old woman and I sleep with the fire between us. In the cold weather when neither the fire nor the blankets are enough to keep us warm we bury ourselves in the sand — right up to the neck.

That is the way my forefathers stayed alive in the millenia before blankets and billies came to this country.

Barney is proud of his river, his clean white hair, and his fish.

Who wouldn't be? But I wonder how long Barney would live and stay clean if he had to hunt for his food in the Wailbri desert and find water in underground soaks?

A full belly encourages sloth, my friend, and causes the wind to blow and the tongue to rattle. The Wailbri tribesmen, who never have full bellies, have always to be mentally alert in order to catch enough food to stay alive.

We are too preoccupied with the pressing business of survival to worry about what neighbours might think of the way we live.

Here is a strange thing: The Nangomeri on the Daly River, in the land of soapflakes and barramundi, are dying out. About fifty of them remain.

The Wailbri, in the land of sand and snakes, are multiplying. Our tribe now numbers more than one thousand and is growing.

Maybe that's because we are not being washed away.

> I saw the black man 'neath a mulga tree,
> Body earth-stained and blending with the sea
> Of spinifex stems that swayed upon the sand.
> And as I looked it somehow seemed that he
> Was part of this red rugged desert land.

His hair was knotted as a matted ring
Of clay and grease bound tight with bush-made string,
A hunting aid to help him stalk his prey.
And as he cooked his food I heard him sing
A low harsh chant to dreamlands far away.

He watched me as I rode up to his tree,
And as he smiled his old eyes questioned me.
I gave the sign of 'Water' to imply
That this I craved. And, rising, wordless, he
Beckoned, and pointed to a soak nearby.

Quite silently, beside an old ghost gum
He showed me liquid, 'neath a layer of scum.
And thirstily I drank from blood-red ground,
And drinking felt as one who, deaf and dumb,
Has heard at last the song of earthly sound.

The Bearded Lady

PITJENTJARRA TRIBE

CENTRAL AUSTRALIA

←———————————————————————

LET ME ASSURE YOU THAT there are few aboriginal women who can grow a beard. I'm one of the fortunate and I'm proud of it.

In the Pitjentjarra tribe a beard represents strength and majesty whether it's worn by a man or woman. I wouldn't shave it off for all the goannas in the desert.

I'm well aware that my moustache, my misshapen mouth, my watering eyes and my mouse-eaten hair are not quite beautiful, but I have other attributes which might convince you that beauty is more than skin deep. In any case, they have won me a lot of respect in the tribe.

The chief of these, as with most aboriginal women, are courage, fortitude, stoicism, and an unquenchable will to ensure the survival of the tribe in face of overwhelming difficulties.

It was in the time of the Big Drought which lasted five years. Thousands of square miles of our tribal land was a sea of molten red powder — the bare, denuded soil. The trees were dead or dying or had been broken down and eaten by the starving cattle. Even the bull-spinifex had been pawed out of the ground and eaten down to the roots. Kangaroos died in millions, the cattle in thousands, the people in hundreds.

Many of the aboriginals — the Aranda, the Loritja, the Pitjentjarra and the Wailbri — waited until the waters had dried up before attempting to cross the No Man's Land to the sustenance offered at mission stations and government settlements. Then it was too late, but still they went.

I was one who crossed the great sandy desert with my two young boys.

49

My husband was blind, stricken with trachoma, emaciated by malnutrition, his mouth bleeding from scurvy. I led him at the other end of a stick until one day he fell flat on his face and was dead when I turned around. I watched the kite-hawks circling, waiting for us to move on before gorging in his poisoned flesh.

I walked ninety miles with my two boys, aged nine and eleven. The average daily temperature was 110 degrees. Water on the track had vanished. We carried just enough to keep us going but never enough to quench our intolerable thirsts.

I had recently had another baby which died. In my breasts I still had milk. I forced my two boys to suckle, to draw from me the strength that would keep them going — for most of the natural food had vanished with the water. I found witchetty grubs in the bark of trees. I showed them where to dig for yams. Once we ate the flesh of a stenching rabbit.

I collapsed a mile from the mission on the sixth day. We had walked slowly because we were weak. My last conscious thought was to give the boys their direction. Then I crawled into the shade of a mulga bush to die.

The missionary came later that day. He strapped me to his camel, gave me water and goat's milk, and led me to the settlement, where I revived.

There were hundreds of similar stories. I'm not boasting when I tell you mine. I was simply trying to show that the hereditary endurance of aboriginal women can be more important than their beauty.

Native and white man alike are frightened of the drought when it combines forces with the desert. A recent one has lasted for six years. I have lived to see the country in which I almost perished suffering again from Big Drought. Communications are better now. Wireless transceivers are everywhere, roads have been fire-ploughed, and aerodromes built. Only a foolish person need die of thirst. But it hurts me to look at my tribal land. I see it blowing away, the topsoil being scattered to mix with the sands in the Simpson Desert. I have a six-year-old grandson who has never seen green grass or water running in a creek. Maybe he will see them next year; for when the rain comes the country is transformed almost overnight. The green shoots sprout within a few days. The dry soil takes a large share of the first waters, but then the creeks run and the children play in red mud.

Yes, maybe next year . . . we have been saying that for six long years. We are sure each time we say it that the rain cannot be much longer delayed . . . and yet there are no clouds. I think our tribal rainmaker needs a new set of rubbing stones.

Author's Footnote: The rains came. At Singleton station near Tennant Creek ten inches fell in two days, and twenty inches in a week. This was more rain than the country had seen in the previous five years. Tanks seven feet tall were under water. Rubber boats were paddled along bush tracks. Fowls roosted in the trees for two days. Fish were caught in the middle of the Stuart Highway at Bonney Creek . . . a week after two aboriginal children perished from thirst. We threw the rainmaker's stones in the river.

Ted Cooper

IWAIJA TRIBE

DARWIN, N.T.

← ———————————————————————————

YOU ARE WONDERING WHY Anita and Patricia appear so disdainful? So would you, Mister, if your Dad had just said he would drive you down to the corner shop for double-headed icecreams and then along comes a pernickety photographer who wants them to pose patiently.

What they are thinking can be summed up in two words: Hurry Up!

Anita has missed out on her daily icecream since yesterday. It will be two days tomorrow since Patricia had hers. If there is anything an aboriginal child likes better than an icecream it is two icecreams.

So shake it up, Mister. Let that dicky-bird out.

Don't get the idea that because aboriginal children like icecream that we haven't got tribal delicacies, too. There are many of them, starting with Sugarbag, which is wild honey. This is a delicious sweet that we find in hollow tree trunks.

All our delicacies are natural foods. None of them are manufactured, like icecream and lollies. Witchetty grubs are well known. So are turtle eggs. Others are rarer but equally delicious. In our tribal country around the Cobourg Peninsula, for instance, there is an enormous harvest of mud oysters and mud crabs. The oysters are so big that they have to be cut; only a glutton would attempt to put a whole one in his mouth. The mud crabs, weighing several pounds, are regarded as a delicacy even by white people, and are said to be better than lobster.

Have you ever tried crocodile eggs? They're scrumptious. They're about the size of a goose egg. Roast one in the ashes, then knock the top off and eat it with your fingers. Oh boy! Unfortunately, in some tribes they are taboo to children. The old men regard them as 'hard' tucker. They want the full supply themselves, so they adopt the simple expedient of putting them under taboo. Make no mistake that the taboo is observed; one boy who defied it and was found out was later eaten by a crocodile.

Stingray Pie? Possum Pie? Baked Bandicoot? Turtle Egg Omelette? Ah, turtle eggs are supreme. There are about sixty in a nest, all with soft shells. We use the shells as a kind of chewing gum, masticating and expelling them in a long stream long after the egg itself has been eaten.

My name is Ted Cooper, formerly of the Iwaija tribe, now a fully-fledged Australian citizen. These are my children.

This citizenship business is a bit of a lark. A few years ago the Government decided that some aboriginal men in the Northern Territory were ready to mix on equal terms with the white Australians.

I was one of them. We became what are technically known as 'non-wards.' The remaining sixteen thousand from Darwin to Alice Springs, from the Western Australian border to Queensland, were declared to be 'wards.'

In practice this means that the citizens — the 'non-wards' — can do as they like within the law.

They can even act like white men.

But within limits.

A white citizen, for instance, can give any mate of his a drink of beer.

We are prevented from giving our mates a drink because they are not citizens.

The penalty for doing so used to be six months in Fanny Bay gaol, without the option of a fine.

Citizen Bruce Pott went to gaol because he gave non-citizen Jackie-woodiebung a drink of beer.

The late citizen Albert Namatjira went to gaol because he gave non-citizen Henoch Raberaba a drink of rum.

This kind of thing can be confusing, especially if my wife, Margaret, should hand around Christmas pudding and brandy sauce.

Most of our guests would have to go without the sauce.

However, enough of such politics. A generation from now we will have forgotten that such problems existed.

My chief interest in life, apart from my family, is the Wanderers Football Club, of which I have been captain.

I am addicted to Australian Rules football like Anita and Patricia are addicted to icecream. I just can't get it out of my system — and, frankly, I'm not trying very hard.

The Wanderers is a team made up mainly of fullblood friends of mine who live in the Darwin area.

We play against white teams every week. I must say that on the sporting field we seldom find any trace of the racial prejudice which is so unfortunate a part of our normal lives.

The fellers in the white teams are wonderful chaps who play hard but fairly and treat us as other sportsmen.

I think it's a pity we can't be treated as sportsmen throughout the week — and not just on Saturdays.

Wonggu

I NOW SMOKE THE PIPE of peace with the white man, but for thirty years I waged unrelenting war against him and the yellow man.

I am Wonggu Balang of the Jabu tribe from the remote north-eastern corner of the vast Arnhem Land reserve.

The white man has sometimes called me King Wonggu. That is wrong because there are no kings among the aboriginal people. He has also sometimes called me Wonggu the Murderer, but I cannot understand how he justifies the name when none of his own courts has convicted me.

To the Japanese pearl fishermen and trepangers I was known as Wonggu the Wicked. But I wonder who was wicked?

Our people had a private trading agreement with the Japanese. Fishermen who came five thousand miles from Japan in small boats and were away from home for nine months felt the need for women's company long before they were due to return. The only women on the coast were jet-black aborigines.

The Arnhemlanders had been introduced to the white man's narcotics and were beset by terrible cravings if the supply of tobacco was cut off.

Therefore let us be frank about it: We had women and the Japanese had tobacco and a brisk trade was undoubtedly done.

Say, if you like, that we established the most primitive call-girl business in the world.

It was strictly against the rules for the Japanese to associate with our women, so it all had to be done surreptitiously. We welcomed them when the coast was clear with a series of flares. If a government patrol boat was known to be in the area we warned them off with other signals.

We traded thus, happily, for years. Occasionally they treated us to lugger parties at which saki flowed like water and the strum of samisen joined the primitive didgeredoo in lending background music to the languor and naughtiness of our assignations. Inevitably, half-caste Japanese-aboriginal children were born.

We might have been trading happily still, but as the war approached the Japanese became arrogant and truculent. They demanded more than they gave. We were not getting a fair exchange. Grievances developed and, in the way of my people, were nurtured and exaggerated.

Then one lugger sailed off to Japan with several of our comeliest women aboard. They were abducted. We have no proof of this but we have heard that they did not reach Japan. Instead, they were thrown overboard when they had outlived their usefulness.

Primitive men thus deprived of their wives can be capable of much cunning determination to equal the score. My tribesmen gathered at Caledon Bay and waited for two luggers to drop anchor. They watched closely as the Japanese came ashore to cure their trepang in smoke-houses on the beach.

So we had our revenge. Tanaka was the first to be transfixed — by a spear. Kimishimi fell with a shovel-blade protruding from his back. Shibasaki ran for the dinghy and was speared at the water's edge. Higasaki tried to swim back to the lugger but our tribesman, Noming, caught him and split his skull with a stone axe. Inamore hid in the bush, but we caught him there and the execution was brief. One man alone, Anki Kinjo, escaped our retribution. He walked one hundred miles to the mission station with foreign natives from his crew.

The white man told us we mustn't kill and sent many of my people to gaol. Then, in 1942, they came to us and said, 'Wonggu, suppose you and your mob see any Japanese here, you kill them all quick-time.'

'But what about gaol?' I asked.

'Never mind the gaol,' they said. 'We'll give you a medal instead.'

I have one other claim to fame. In my day I was a great artist. I mixed my own paints with red and yellow ochre and white clay. I painted on bark, and I painted on the walls of caves, a successor to those primitive artists from the Time of Dream who painted the paths of our culture in caves and on rocks throughout the land; the painters about whom the poet wrote:

> On Ober's plain we saw the grey mist rise
>   Out of the reed-lagoon at early dawn,
> And heard the brolgas calling from the skies
>   As others danced to greet the coming morn.
>
> We tramped through buffalo grass, and on the range
>   Behind the jungle, where the leichhardts stand,
> We marvelled as we looked upon the strange
>   Primeval cave-art of this ancient land.
>
> And gazing thus our thoughts were on this place,
>   Its people with their ritual and their lore.
> Legends on stone! The story of a race
>   That fades away as time sweeps all before.
>
> Sweeps all before! Traditions, rituals die,
>   Only the aged to their customs cling,
> Peering around with dim and wondering eye
>   When mission youth goes forth as church bells ring.
>
> The old and new . . . and time goes on its way
>   As we return across green Ober's plain.
> The sun, a gleaming coal, lights up the day,
>   Reflecting on the ochred porcelain.

Sunworshippers

ARANDA TRIBE

CENTRAL AUSTRALIA

←————————————————————————————

WE ARE THREE OLD sunworshippers from the Aranda tribe on the Finke River in Central Australia. We can't give you our names because nudism – the white man's word for it – is against his law.

Although we lived like this for generations we can be arrested and thrown into gaol if we do so in public.

Therefore we are forced to wear The Boss's cast-off clothes. It makes us self-conscious. We would prefer to remain just like this. What's the point in wearing trousers if you have nothing to put in the pockets?

There are some white men who prefer to see us naked, especially our women. They are the photographers, and people who pose as photographers.

We had a little discussion with one of them recently. The conversation went like this:

Photographer: I say, your women are getting a bit uppity, aren't they?

Us: Perhaps so, sir. Of what do you complain? (Or words to that effect.)

Photographer: Well, I was coming out here the other day and I saw a big buck nigger and his gin. This gin, she had big tits, whoppers they were, real blockbusters, and I thought she'd make a good picture, maybe I'd be able to sell it to one of those blokes who writes books, so I told her to take her clothes off, I mean you can't have a good picture of a gin clobbered up with clothing. And you know what?

Us: What?

Photographer: She wouldn t. She would not take her clothes off for me.

Us: Yes. Well, we must admit they're getting uppity all right. Won't take their clothes off when they're asked. That's a little unreasonable. By the way, sir, is that your wife with you?

Photographer: Yes.

Us: Well, sir, we have a camera — just an old Box Brownie; neverthe-less, a camera. We were wondering, sir, if you would tell you wife to take her clothes off while we photograph her? Will that be all right?

Photographer: All right be blowed! What are you coming at?

Us: But, sir . . .

Photographer: But nothing! I can see you're getting a bit uppity, too; you niggers are all the same.

Mind you, clothes do have their compensations. Some of our tribesmen who wear shirts and trousers find they stop sunburn.

What's that? You thought black skins were immune from sunburn? Don't you believe it.

It is not so visible as on a white skin, which turns pink, but we suffer just the same. Some of our people are more allergic than others. That's why you occasionally see them wearing heavy overcoats on a hot day. They say that an overcoat keeps the heat out.

Perhaps you also think that like the Negroes and the Orientals we all have black hair? Don't believe that, either.

The Aranda, Pitjentjarra, Loritja and Wailbri tribes all have a percent-age of blondes, especially among the women and children. Their hair is quite fair, as though it's been bleached in the sun.

But to get back to nudism: in our opinion it is the ultimate in bodily freedom. There is no greater pleasure than to have the sun and the wind caressing one's entire body.

We save time in not having to undress on the way to bed, and to be ready for the day the moment we get up. And think of the money we save on laundry and dry-cleaning bills, not to mention the capital outlay for suits, shirts, shoes, hats, dresses, stockings — and fur coats for the women.

We are three Elders of the Aranda. It is through us, the Old Men, that the sacred laws and legends are passed down from generation to generation.

We are the tribal rulers, the masters of the ceremonial, the teachers of tradition — and the dictators of fashion!

If we go naked the rest of the tribe goes naked, too. If one of us wears a shirt without trousers you'd be surprised how quickly this fad is copied by others.

They tell us that white people are equally conformist in this way. Let a Princess wear a certain pillbox hat and in no time similar hats appear on millions of heads throughout the world. Let the wife of a President wear a particular hair-style and it is affected overnight by every coiffeur worth his salt.

A strange business, indeed. Wouldn't it solve many problems if we all agreed to wear only the garment which clothed us at birth — the skin?

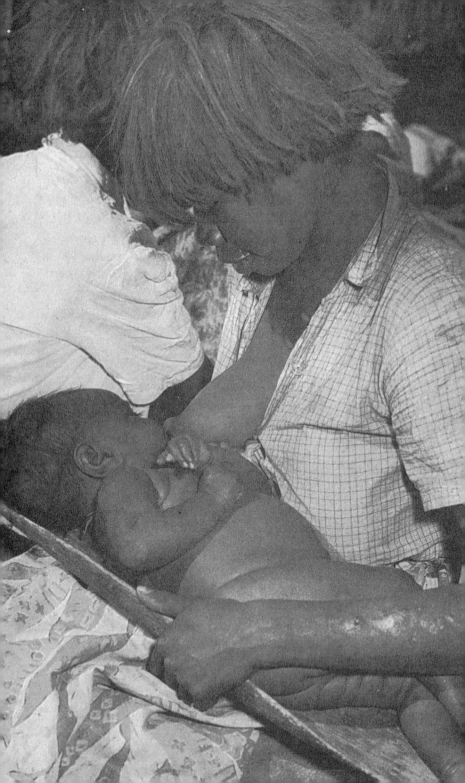

Baby Matthew

WAILBRI TRIBE

CENTRAL AUSTRALIA

←——————————————————————————

One night beside a campfire's glow
I heard a Songman chanting low
A song of life. And overhead
The stars gleamed bright, and this he said:

Life is a day, and as the dawn
Comes from the earth, a child is born.
Grim night departs, dawn lights the sky,
And with it comes the infant's cry.

      The earth-ones give,
      The wise ones know
      The tribes shall live
      As children grow.

The sun comes up, so grows the child,
Meekly at first, then strong and wild,
Noisy as birds that sweep and cry
That strong ones live as weak ones die.

      Thus children play,
      For Elders know
      Strength comes to they
      Who thrive and grow.

The day grows bright, the sun is strong,
So grows the youngster sleek and strong,
And as a tree spreads strong with shade,
The Elders meet and a man is Made.

The totems give,
The Elders know
The tribe shall live
As children grow.

There's one thing about black mothers: they give white milk. . . .

My Mummy loves me just as much as any white mother; perhaps more, in fact.

She is not obliged to waste a lot of mushy love on my Daddy, and is thus able to give it all to me.

The relationship between fathers and mothers in the Wailbri tribe is undemonstrative. My Mum and Dad have a deep affection for each other but I've never heard them whispering sweet nothings in the dark.

The moon in June on the silver lagoon doesn't mean anything in their love lives. They're not likely to talk about the fine texture of black hair, the smoothness of black skin, or the depth of black eyes.

If he wants to demonstrate affection my Dad gives my Mum a few puffs at his pipe. She might scoop a hiphole in the sand for him, or bring him a piece of grilled lizard for his dinner.

They do not kiss. The thought of doing so would be abhorrent to them. They stroke one another gently and murmur softly when they feel the physical need of each other.

I'm not supposed to know about these things but there's not much privacy in an aborigines' camp.

We have only one wind break, one fire, and one blanket each. We huddle together to keep warm in winter. Mum often has to get up to stoke the fire, and it's then that I see her crawl back into my Dad's blanket.

I hope you don't think I was conceived and born as the result of sexual intercourse which takes place there.

Some of the sophisticated natives in Alice Springs say that a man can give a woman a child in this way.

But we know better than that. My Mum and Dad know that I was created by a spirit entering her body.

You laugh? Nonsense, you say?

Yet I heard you say you were a Christian. If that is so, you must believe in virgin birth, in immaculate conception.

Then why laugh at us if we think babies are formed by spirit children who pass into the mother while she sleeps? All true Christians believe that. And so did the Ancient Greeks.

By the way, my name is Matthew. My mother's name is Dora Nambidjimba. We live two hundred miles north-west of Alice Springs, on the fringe of the Great Sandy Desert.

If you want to argue the point with us about how conception takes place in a woman, why not come out here to see us at Yuendumu settlement?

We could give you a windbreak and a fire and we'd find a spare blanket for you.

Or do you believe that babies are found under cabbages?

Tiger

LORITJA TRIBE

CENTRAL AUSTRALIA

←———————————————————————————————

MY HANDSOME CLASSICALLY aboriginal features have won me a job as tourist guide for a bus company at a resort not more than five hundred miles from Alice Springs.

But I'm there not only as a guide: Part of my job is to convince the tourists that they're getting what they paid for.

Like it said in the glossy brochures . . . 'See the wild grandeur of Central Australia . . . see the primitive aborigines in their natural habitats . . . see them throwing spears and boomerangs as they hunt for their food.' Ad nauseum.

So I'm here to give them their money's worth. For, confidentially, in the off-season you wouldn't see a blackfeller within a hundred miles.

Why would we want to live here, in all this isolation, when we can be in Alice Springs or at one of the government settlements? We're not that dumb. Frankly, I wouldn't be here during the tourist season, either, except that the company makes it worth my while.

In fact I get it both ways: I'm on the payroll with Rough-It Tours, and I also take the tourists for sizable lumps of cold cash. How? Well, I'll tell you.

You must remember that most tourists who come to the inland are on Their Big Adventure. They've always thought of Alice Springs and The Centre as being at the back of beyond.

Then suddenly they decide to leave the suburban street and come on one of these Rough-Its, with three-course meals three times a day, refrigerators everywhere they stop, iced drinks, swimming pools, pretty hostesses, and never so much as a folding stretcher to destroy the monotony of inner-spring mattresses. Finally, after plenty of build-up, they arrive here at The Gorge. As they drive up I can hear the loudspeaker in the bus (I've been rehearsed in all this, of course) and the driver is saying: 'If you watch carefully you might just be lucky enough to see a primitive aboriginal, a Stone-Age man, hunting game.'

That's my cue. I jump out from behind a bush and streak across the flat, throwing boomerangs and spears at imaginary kangaroos and — in five minutes or so — coming back to camp suitably empty-handed.

'Oh, you poor man,' they say. 'How long is it since you had a good meal?' (Actually I had steak and eggs for lunch in the staff dining room.)

'Oh, what a shame,' they say, 'that you have no clothes!' (Yes, I'm wearing only a narga. My shirt and trousers are in the wardrobe.)

But I tell them the hard times and my starving wife and kids up in the hills. I say I haven't speared a kangaroo for three days. And I wait for the reactions.

After a while one of the men will come over. Surreptitiously he hands me a pound note. A woman gives me ten shillings. Occasionally there's a fiver. And so it goes.

'Fancy meeting a real primitive in his authentic surroundings,' they say. 'Just like it said in the brochures.'

Naturally they're all laden with cameras and this is too good an opportunity for them to miss.

'Could I take your photograph?' one asks.

Yes, sir, I tell him. Two shillings for every exposure. The correct setting for colour film is f.8 at 1/50th of a second. They seem a little surprised at that, but they queue-up as I pose and I get two-bob from each.

After that they want pictures of me throwing spears. Two bob, sir.

And throwing boomerangs. Two bob, sir.

'Can you make fire by rubbing sticks together?' Yes, sir. Two bob.

You'd be surprised how it adds up. It's not a bad racket at all. Now pardon me; here comes another bus.

Incidentally, this kind of tourism is now beginning in reverse. There was a time when itchy-feet among my people meant nothing more than that they went on Walkabout.

But today an increasing number are saving their money and going south to see the big cities.

It all began when the government sent a few men to Royal Shows in various states to explain aboriginal artifacts to the masses. There was time for extracurricular sight-seeing: the Sydney Harbour Bridge, the underground railway, the Melbourne Cricket Ground, the big steamers, the big trains, the trams, and the buildings hundreds of feet tall.

We get fun from watching city tourists who come out here, and prove to us in a few moments that they've never been in the bush in their lives.

But the city-slickers must get equally as much fun from explaining their wonders to the hayseed aborigines.

You should have heard the lying stories these men told when they returned! One of them told me he had seen red, white and blue electric lights flashing on and off without anyone controlling a switch. He also said he'd seen a sign with lights running around the outside.

Another man said he went into a building that was higher than fifty big mulga trees. A door was shut, a switch was pressed, the door opened — and he was on top of the building *without walking!*

One man wanted me to believe that in a big shop they have a ladder which moves up and down. The people stand on it and are taken from one floor to another. He also said he saw cars parked in houses fifty feet above the roadway.

But of all the liars I've ever heard, that old Jack Kelly (whose picture is in this book) is the worst. He wanted me to believe there was a bridge with hundreds of cars crossing it at once, and trains, too. Old Jack is incorrigible.

Jumbo and Wally

WAILBRI TRIBE

CENTRAL AUSTRALIA

←————————————————————————

Not monuments to some king's vanished glory,
But flints and chards record man's greatest story.
Some husks and shells beside the grinding stones,
A painted cave, or etchings scratched on bones.
The debris on the floor of sheltering caves,
Or where erosion throws up ancient graves.
There find the story of that lowly one
Who first made fire, he who made that sun
To cast aside night's horror, set man free
To conquer unknown lands, to brave the sea.
Out of that misty past great things were wrung
By unknown heroes who have died unsung.
Speech, ritual, fire, iron and the wheel,
Crops sown and reaped and ground to give us meal.
Each creature of this earth from horse to bee
They conquered in that so-called savagery.
How great that history when the tales begin
Amidst the ashes of our primal kin.
To follow slowly down the changing years
Their trials, hopes, disasters, doubts and fears.
Our laws, religion, customs, all were born
Amidst the chards and flints of mankind's dawn.
Dig deep, O Spade, beneath the pomp of kings
To search amidst the dust for great small things.

73

I say, mister, have you got a match? Thanks awfully.

A man could die of nicotine starvation sometimes while he's trying to make fire to light a cigarette.

We are Jumbo Jabaldjari and Old Wally Jabaldjari, Wailbri tribal brothers at Yuendumu settlement out from Alice Springs.

We have made fire since The Dreamtime in this way — by rubbing two pieces of wood together until the friction produces heat, then smoke, and finally flame when a tinder is applied.

Even today, mid-way through the twentieth century, we still do not use matches. Why? Because matches cost money and friction costs nothing. We have no money but plenty of friction.

It is possible, of course, for one man alone to make fire by twirling a stick between his palms until the heat produced against another piece of wood first smokes and then blazes.

But this is an easier way: we sit facing one another with an upturned shield on the ground and the edge of a woomera in a slot on the shield.

We apply downward pressure and move the woomera back and forth, like two men using a crosscut saw. Slowly at first, then faster and faster as the smoke shows and we apply a dry tinder of powdered wood or leaves.

How long does it take? We can kindle flame in fifteen seconds.

Perhaps it was our ancestors who first produced fire. It is certain that when they arrived in Australia during the Pleistocene Age they brought no safety matches with them.

Whoever our ancestors were — Dravidians from India or just plain monkeys — they must have been cold until they taught themselves a few of the tricks we now know.

Did it happen accidentally when sparks flew off wooden weapons wielded by two fighting men?

Did they see the bush set on fire by lightning and experiment with their primitive implements until they had duplicated the effect?

Did the sun shine on a piece of glass or tin until the heat thus created set fire to nearby grass? No; because they had neither glass nor tin nor any other metal. They had only wood and stone.

We don't do this kind of thing every day. Once our campfire is burning it is never allowed to go out. Someone has to stoke it during the night. When rain falls we bury the coals in sand and retrieve them, still red hot, when it clears.

If we move camp we take a firestick with us. Actually, we are doing this now for that damn-fool Douglas Lockwood, who has a box of safety matches and a cigarette lighter in his pocket. How do we know? Because we've seen their outline against his trousers. What he doesn't know is that in a minute he is going to provide us with both matches and tobacco.

Those scars on Wally's back? Thereby hangs a tale long enough to fill this and several other books.

Wally was a bit of a Romeo in his youth and also a great fighting man. Each one of those scars was inflicted separately by men who had been cuckolded. As you can see, some of them are nine inches long and very deep. In those days we had no medicines and no bandages other than mud and bark.

But Wally recovered each time. What about his tormentors?

Confidentially, some of them acquired cuts which began on the back and came out through the chest.

The Swimming Hole

GUNWINGGU TRIBE

WEST ARNHEM LAND

←————————————————————→

WHAT MORE COULD ANY boy ask for than this: a swimming hole and a diving board both provided by nature?

Line up for your dive, swim to the bank, scamper up the fallen tree trunk, dive again . . . until boredom sets in.

But boredom seldom troubles us here. The mighty stream flowing below us is the East Alligator River, which forms part of the western boundary of the thirty thousand square miles Arnhem Land reserve.

Why do you think it is called East Alligator?

Because it is full of man-eating crocodiles. Nearby are the South Alligator and West Alligator. All are favoured spots by professional crocodile shooters.

Allow us to digress for a moment: Crocodile shooting is now a very lucrative business. The hides are worth twenty shillings an inch, measured around the widest part of the belly. A big one, therefore, is worth about forty pounds.

Most of the shooting is done at night with spotlights. Have you ever been in a dugout canoe on a remote river on a black-as-pitch night and seen the red eyes of a crocodile reflected in a spotlight's beam? Now that's what we call sinister and spine-tingling. Real scary. You know that not far away a prehistoric monster is watching you, and if you don't get him first and your canoe is upset the chances are that he will get you.

We leave that to our fathers. They glide up quietly to the tell-tale eyes. The crocodiles are hypnotised by the light. When they are a few feet away

77

one of the men throws a sharply pointed harpoon. The crocodile is hit behind the ear, and is soon dead. It is dragged to the shore, where it is skinned and the hide salted. That is a tedious, back-breaking business, and it is generally done in a place where there are millions of mosquitoes and sandflies.

And, almost without exception, the river banks are lined with deep, oozy mud. Other crocodiles may be lurking there.

Now you know why we are not bothered with ennui.

Every time we dive in there is a chance that we may not come up. One of the big fellows might be waiting down there with his arms and jaws open in welcome.

A twenty-five footer would need only two bites to dispose of any one of us.

He'd regard us as hors d'œuvres.

Hence the eternal warning from our parents when we go to swim: 'The crocodiles will get you if you don't watch out.'

But a feller can't chicken-out when all his mates are diving in. Nevertheless, we are constantly on the alert for tell-tale bubbles which would betray a crocodile's presence.

We never dive in until we have watched the surface of the muddy opaque water for half an hour. If there have been no air bubbles in that time and there are no tracks in the mud on the bank we feel reasonably safe.

The sense of danger is, of course, just what we want. It adds the spice that every boy looks for in his games. There is a certain thrill in the knowledge that at any moment a playful monster might tickle your toes or shorten you by a foot.

See that little feller sitting on the diving board? His father, Micky, was attacked by a fifteen footer while swimming across the river. It grabbed him with its claws and dragged him under while Micky tried to keep out of the way of the snapping jaws and flashing teeth.

He hammered at its eyes with his fists and thumbs until it released him.

Then he was in such a hurry he almost walked on top of the water to the bank.

Micky was badly scarred and had to be taken to Darwin hospital. But he would never have been seen again if the crocodile had managed to reach him with its jaws.

He was very frightened yet philosophic about it all. We often eat crocodile flesh out here so we couldn't blame the crocodile for wanting to eat one of us.

'That time 'gator nearly get level-feller,' Micky says.

One Pound Jimmy

←————————————————————————————————————

SOME PEOPLE CALL ME Australia because that's the name they gave me on the postage stamp.

Actually it is One Pound Jimmy, although you can see for yourself that I'm worth only two and sixpence. In the Wailbri tribe they call me Gwoja Jungarai.

Not a bad profile, eh? Eyes deeply set behind the shaggy brows to protect them from the vertical rays of the Central Australian sun.

A broad nose, classically aboriginal. The better to smell you with, as one of our hunters said to a fat kangaroo.

A fine flowing beard, pointed nicely to hide my receding chin. It's a trick I learnt from some of the bluebloods.

Frankly, my beard is purely a utility affair. I wouldn't wear it at all if we had plenty of water in the desert and I carried a hand-towel. But out here, three hundred miles west of Alice Springs, things are inclined to be dry and dirty.

You need something to wipe your hands on after a greasy meal of goanna. Hence the beard.

Notice how my hair is tied with a braid? That's an old trick of the tribal hunters. When you've been stalking an animal for hours — perhaps days — and you're ravenously hungry, you don't want to lose him just because your long hair waves in the breeze at the wrong moment, or blows in your eyes as you take aim with a shovel-nose spear. It's far too long between meals in this country for that to happen twice.

I'm very proud of this picture and of the fact that I'm the only aboriginal ever to have had his face engraved on a postage stamp.

The Postmaster-General didn't pick Albert Namatjira, who was a famous painter.

He didn't pick Robert Tudawali, who was a film star.

He picked me because he wanted a rugged handsome face.

Not before time, either, that my people were honoured by having an aboriginal face on a stamp.

The first postage stamp was printed in Great Britain in 1840, although there had been a system of regular mail services in the seventeenth century. It might surprise you to know, therefore, that we have had systems of passing messages and the rather modern refinement of Registered Post for centuries.

Anybody who reads comics knows all about smoke signals, a form of bush wireless that has always been used by my people.

The cartoonists would have you believe that smoke-signalling is a refined method of communicating messages over long distances. That is nonsense. I have never known smoke to mean anything other than the publication of a man's whereabouts.

Tribal country is sacrosanct. We don't have passports or visas, but we do have our primitive equivalents of them. It would be a flagrant breach of diplomatic manners for a Wailbri tribesman to hunt on Pintubi land, or even to trespass there without good reason. Any man walking through the land of another tribe, therefore, sends up smoke signals to let the locals know of his approach. It is one of the courtesies we observe. Wars have been declared in the past because of unauthorized invasion of territory by the black as well as the white tribes of the earth.

Tribal groups seeing smokes approaching know that they are about to be visited by the representatives of other tribes. On clear days, such smokes can be seen up to one hundred miles away, which means about three days travel. A man who advertises himself by smoke is generally welcomed at his destination. But one who keeps his presence secret is inclined to be regarded as a spy. In the old days he would almost certainly have ended with a spear between his shoulder blades.

Smoke is well known as one of our means of communication.

However, not many have heard of our infallible system of delivering messages and goods over enormous distances. This is done by using a message stick, like the one Dambu Milburr is carving on the next page.

I might want to send tobacco and other presents to my son who is working with a drover hundreds of miles away. I wait until I find a blackfellow who is going his way. That might take weeks or months but time is something we have plenty of in this country. The mails don't close every day.

These goods would normally not reach their destination. The postie would smoke the tobacco and give the presents to his own friends.

But once I have given him the message stick I know that the goods will be delivered just as certainly as if I had a Registered Packet receipt from the P.M.G.

They'd better be. Otherwise I'd have his kidney fat as compensation.

Dambu Milburr

MAIKULAN TRIBE

MORNINGTON ISLAND, GULF OF CARPENTARIA

My old boss big gov'ment man,
  Sit longa chair and write all day;
Talk longa girl that write shorthan'
  'Nother-one man take letter away.

Letter come in and letter go out,
  My old boss 'im talk, write, talk;
Finish 'im job, can't walkabout,
  Must have car for 'im no-like walk.

But here am I writing letters in *my* office, without a secretary to take dictation, without a mailman, and without a car to take me home when I'm tired. I hate writing letters but I'm so far behind with my correspondence that I must catch up.

I have been writing all morning and have used three small trees, but still I'm not finished. Talk about Moses and his Tablets of Stone!

When the white man writes a letter he does so with paper and ink or a writing machine he calls a typewriter. (Trust him to make it easy for himself.)

But when we write letters we do it with a knife and a piece of softwood. They are called Message Sticks.

Sometimes it takes me half a day to finish one and even then it contains only a couple of sentences.

The worst that can happen to a white letter writer is that he gets his fingers covered in ink.

The worst that can happen to me is that unless I'm very careful I may cut off my thumb or index finger.

The trouble is that my blood is tribally sacred, and when it spills I have to pay a fine. If my shirt is stained with the blood it is almost certain that the shirt will be taken from me by a relative who considers himself injured. How do you like that! I'm wounded — but he's injured! Or they might take the pocket-knife or razor with which the wound was inflicted. In recent years I have lost dozens of shirts, knives and razors in this way. In one of our ceremonials my blood is used for sticking feathers to the bodies of my tribesmen, and for ornamenting their weapons. Each ceremony requires about a jamtinful. Sometimes it has to be watered down to make enough. The backs of my arms and legs are scarred with cuts where I have opened veins for my relatives. They don't mind me doing this when they want blood, but if I spill it accidentally while writing a letter I have to pay up.

And quite often after I've finished a letter I can't understand my own writing and have to do it again.

In fact, I'm having the greatest difficulty reading the message I've just written. You can see that from the puzzled look on my face.

Actually this is a long overdue letter to my mother. I know a man who is walking out to where she lives, so I thought I would send along a letter with a few presents.

After all that leg-pulling I suppose I had better tell the truth.

The message stick we use is not really a letter.

It serves purely as a reminder to the carrier of the messages he has to deliver verbally, just as though it was a piece of string tied around the finger or knots in the corner of a handkerchief.

Old One Pound Jimmy — that boaster whose face appeared on the postage stamp — has said that it also acts as a kind of registered post.

That is true, but it also acts as a passport through foreign country and identifies the courier to a recipient.

86

The notches I have cut in my stick will be explained in detail to the postman who is going to my mother. The first notch reminds him to tell her that I am well and that all her grandchildren are well.

The second notch is to say that here on Mornington Island we have had an excellent season for dugong, turtle eggs and barramundi.

When he sees the third larger notch the postman will remember to say that I hope my mother is well and that her grandchildren send their respects.

There are some small horizontal lines on the face of the stick which will remind the courier of the presents I have sent for her: a pound of tobacco, a new dress, and an old pipe that I have finished with.

Finally the little flourish at the end will remind him to say that if she has an excess of things she doesn't want, like money, she could send them back with the courier.

I suppose some people will say that this is therefore a begging letter, but from what I've seen of the world I'd say they were fairly common between sons and mothers.

Ah, well, I had better get on with it.

The mail closes at sundown.

Gladys Namagu Daly

MOOLA BOOLA TRIBE

EAST KIMBERLEYS, W.A.

←————————————————————————

I CAN REMEMBER THE old colour-conscious racially-prejudiced blackfellows saying, 'But would you like YOUR daughter to marry a white man?'

Well, I'm one who did.

My name was Gladys Namagu of the Moola Boola tribe near Hall's Creek, North-West Australia. Now it is Mrs. Michael Daly.

That's my husband, Mick, with a plaster over his face. He is a stockman, a horseman, and an overland drover.

We live in the Wide Spaces and the Quiet Places. My home has no walls. There are no chairs, no tables, no lights, no beds, and no other furniture. There is certainly no refrigerator or TV.

But I've got a double swag on the ground, a campfire, the tray of a truck for a table, the moon for a light, and the logs of fallen trees to sit on.

My home moves ten miles every day. Tonight I may sleep with my husband on a blacksoil plain scattered with a few coolibahs and a lot of death adders. Tomorrow night I will be at a stockroute water-bore where I can bathe and wash clothes. The bores, gushing water from the sub-artesian flow, are my bathroom and laundry.

No butcher calls. The beef I eat walks in front of me as part of the mob of a thousand cattle that Mick is droving across the heartland.

The baker is a halfcaste named Joe Craigie who travels with us. He makes only damper and Johnny cakes.

The milk is dry powder, and it comes in tins.

I suppose that my life, by suburban standards, is harsh and ugly. But by the standards of my tribal people it is easy and good.

Not long ago I was a humble aboriginal girl caught in the war of assimilation between the black and white cultures.

I had a long fight against officialdom before I could get permission to marry Mick. The whites didn't want me to marry a white

But I won the fight and was married on New Year's Day. Many white people danced at my wedding. My honeymoon was spent on horseback, riding across the Barkly Tableland. My bridal suite was a double swag on the ground beneath a desert oak.

I'm the only fullblood in Mick's camp. The others are coloureds or whites. But Mick doesn't stand any funny business. He lets them all know that I am the Boss's Wife, in capital letters. They treat me all right – or look out.

Joe Craigie knows all about that. One night I hit him across the shins with a nulla nulla. Nearly broke his legs. He reckoned I was naughty and smacked me with his hand. So I smacked him – but with a piece of ironwood.

I'll probably stay out here in the never-never all my life. We've got a double bed and mattress back at Wave Hill station, where we pick up the mobs of cattle, but they're only a nuisance.

Who wants a bed when you've got a good warm swag and a few square feet of ground?

Who wants walls when you've got a backdrop of clear blue sky moving ahead of you always?

Who wants furniture when you can do without it?

I defied a tradition when I married outside my tribe into a tribe of a different colour.

The blacks didn't like that. The whites didn't like it much, either.

But Mick and I do.

We fight and we argue, but we have our own brand of rugged happiness.

I'm pleased Mick hasn't got a receipt for me. The classic example of that was the receipt issued by a Djouan tribesman named Charlie Me-ook who, after an evening of convivial but hard bargaining, put his thumb-print to the receipt which follows. To make the names clearer, it should be known that the white man, Charlie Swanson, got his tribal name of Binji-Binji because he weighed 32 stone. The woman he bought weighed seven stone.

RECEIPT

My name Charlie Me-ook. Me belong Djouan tribe of abo-riginal people of the Northern Territory of Australia.

Me savvy Binji-Binji, sometimes called Charlie Swanson, of Maranboy, miner and gardener.

Wife belong me, her name is Ruby Dirriperra.

I don't want her no more.

I now renounce all tribal possession of her and give her to Binji-Binji, whom she has lived with for the past five years, for and in consideration of the said Binji-Binji giving to me in return and exchange for the said Ruby Dirriperra the following:

   150 lbs. of flour.
   70 lbs. of sugar.
    1 lb. of tobacco.

receipt of which is hereby acknowledged on the affixing of my mark at the foot hereof:

Charlie Me-ook   *His Mark.*

I, Ruby Dirriperra, the tribal wife of Charlie Me-ook, am willing to marry in the rites of the Christian religion Binji-Binji, of Maranboy.

Ruby   *Her Mark.*

Ruby Nangala

WAILBRI TRIBE

CENTRAL AUSTRALIA

◀────────────────────────────────────

TAKE ONE LARGE KANGAROO.

Cook it fur and all.

Eat it with your fingers.

All our recipes are fairly simple but Baked Kangaroo is one of the easiest.

I suppose you could say the most difficult part of the operation is the first line: Take one large kangaroo. The kangaroos are never terribly co-operative about being taken, especially by hungry Warramungas and Wailbris.

As they can travel at forty miles an hour and our hunters have to kill them with spears or throwing sticks you can understand that the tribal cooks are sometimes short of meat.

A hunter might stalk a kangaroo for half a day, always down-wind from it, before approaching close enough to throw a spear. In the desert country where we live he is often without adequate natural cover.

The trees are stunted and sparse and Old Man Kangaroos which stand eight feet tall can often keep our men out of spear range.

Little wonder they come home filthy from the hunt. They crawl for miles on their bellies, seldom standing upright until the very moment at which they hurl their spears. I know I always insist on them scrubbing up and changing their nargas before they come to eat in my dining room — even though that is only a squat in the sand around the campfire.

It's no earthly use trying to bake a whole kangaroo in a household stove.

It just won't fit. So I cook mine in the ground as we have done for generations.

I simply scoop out a hole big enough to take the kangaroo, line it with hot stones and coals from the campfire, commit the 'roo to this natural oven, and then cover it entirely with sand.

Cooking time depends on the hunger of the hunters. Occasionally they're willing to wait until I say it is ready — but not often. Normally they're clamouring for food soon after the fur has been scorched. It is certainly underdone.

Yes, I like earth-baked kangaroo except that I've never quite got used to the grit. It sets my teeth on edge.

Another thing: have you ever tried lifting a 100 lb. roasted kangaroo out of an earth oven with your bare hands? I don't recommend it for people with tender skin. I'm pretty tough but it burns the devil out of me.

And, of course, there is always a tribe of kids waiting around for a bone to chew.

Carving is no problem. Each person takes what he wants with his hands. Rather al fresco, I know, but I'm not keen on too much formality. I think that a dish like this would lose its character if we all sat up with our feet under a table, with starched napery and the correct red wine.

What do we drink with our meals? Billy tea or water. There has never been any other drink in our lives, except perhaps a few bottles of lollywater from the canteen at Christmas.

I'm sorry I haven't introduced myself earlier: I'm Ruby Nangala of the East Wailbri tribe. I live at Warrabri settlement near Tennant Creek, Central Australia.

Would you care to stay for lunch? Really, there's plenty for everyone.

No? Well, some other time, perhaps.

Author's Footnote: The Australian bush abounds with kangaroos. In some areas they are a pest. Why not do the pastoralists a favour by putting them on your family's menu. Here are two recipes, for which I am indebted to Bill Harney's Cook Book:

Kangaroo Tail Soup.—Roast the tail in a ground oven (an electric oven will do) or cut it into lengths and bake it in a camp oven (a skillet will do) after scraping off the hair. The skin will come off easily after baking for two to two and a half hours. When the tail has been skinned, cut it into sections and coat it with flour. Put in a cooking pot with water to cover, pepper and salt, a little butter or a portion of bacon, and sliced potatoes, carrots and onions. Let it simmer for one and a half hours, or until the meat starts to leave the bones.

Kangaroo Casserole.—Take a leg of kangaroo (about two pounds weight) and slice the meat into pieces about one-quarter of an inch thick. Cut three or four potatoes into long slices of the same thickness, also three onions and the same quantity of pumpkin. Butter the bottom of the saucepan and put in a layer of kangaroo meat, then a layer of sliced vegetables, then more butter, more meat, more vegetables, alternately, until the pot is almost filled. Then add a little water, about a quarter way up the pot, put it over a quick fire to bring it to the boil, and let it simmer for about three hours. Do not stir, but make sure there is always a little liquid in the pot. The best container for this dish is a tall casserole pot as used in France, but an ordinary saucepan will do. Serves four.°

° Author's Note: Not if I'm there.

George Yenmeni

MURINBADA TRIBE

PORT KEATS, NORTH AUSTRALIA

OUT WHERE I COME from the natives quake with fear when Dead-Eye George Yenmeni the Murderin' Murinbada stalks the streets. They run like rabbits into their warrens. Otherwise they're carried into coffins.

Don't get me wrong, pard. I'm a peaceable enough hombre 'cept when I'm riled. But when I've got me dander up the lead starts flyin' and I calculate some people is more'n likely to get somewhat creased.

Right now, lying here in hospital, a man feels like he's a little de-horsed. You can't do nuthin' much when your shootin' irons is all mixed up with the bedclothes.

I'm used to swingin' the old guns real low where they spring to a man's hand natural-like, and they're spittin' lead just as soon as the muzzles clear those goldarned ole holsters.

I'm not too sure how the ole trigger finger is behavin' right at this minute.

You see, I've been here in this hospital for eight months, run to earth by somethin' these here nurses call polio.

I'm walking down the street at Port Keats mission one day see, swaggerin' away like usual, chasin' all them lily-livered yeller-bellied Muringarrs and Murinjabins down their holes with a truly witherin' fire. All of a sudden the ole legs just pack up on me.

I reckon for a while the Injuns have got me with a poisoned spear but there's nary a thing stickin' outa my hide. No sirree.

Then I reckon might be one of these muskrats has had the gall to draw a gun on Murderin' George of the Murinbada.

No sirree. There ain't no blood anywheres in sight, but still I'm sprawled out in the street and can't get up, like a poleaxed bronco.

Finally Father Leary, the preacher man, comes over to me. A right good hombre this Leary.

'What ails you, Murderin' George?' he says.

'Seems as how the old pins have been shot away,' I says. 'I can't get up.'

It was a bit embarrassin' for the Murderin' Murinbada but the Father picked me up and carried me into the mission hospital, just like if I'da really been croaked.

The Sisters come around and talk with the Father.

'Polio,' I hear them say. Then they talk to Darwin on the pedal radio and the Flying Doctor comes out to see me.

'Murderin' George,' he says, 'we've got to send you down to Adelaide to have steel calipers fitted to these hornery old legs of yourn.'

'That's okay with me, pardner,' I says, 'on one condition, namely: you've got to promise me that I can go every week to see Opperlong Casserty and Roy Rogers and Gene Autry and the goodies and baddies.'

'Done, pard,' he tells me. 'We'll do better than that. We'll get you fixed up with some real fine shootin' irons, and a sombrero, and maybe even a rockin' horse.'

So now I see me ole mate, Oppy, regular. They've patched me up real good with these calipers.

It won't be long now pardner before I'm slingin' a leg over my horse again and going out to plug a dozen of those no-good Murinjabins before breakfast.

Save a few for me until I get there.

You've got to hand it to these missionary fellers like Father Leary; they don't scare easy. Not like them Brinkens. They first came out our way in buckboards, and on horseback.

You don't want to forget, either, that to get here they had to cross some of the worst blackfeller country in Australia. This was the land of Nemarluk and his Red Band, who liked nothing better than killing white men. That was in the days when an S O S had to go into civilization on foot, and help came out the same way. The Flying Doctor Service, roads, and the radio, had then not been thought of.

Nevertheless, they came out and, as though inviting spears in the back, began operations by defying the Elders and urging them to mend their ways. They fought black magic, witchcraft and barbaric cruelties with every rule in the book and a few that weren't, and eventually beat them all with a combination of whitefeller magic and aspirins.

Senile adults and malformed children were buried alive. Ceremonial blood was drunk at initiations. Young girls who did not submit as wives to ugly old men were killed. You-all know the story of Bishop F. X. Gsell, the polygamist priest who acquired 150 'wives' to save them from horrible deaths. They were runaway girls who didn't want their promised husbands. Gsell placated the tribal wrath by buying them for an average of two pounds each in trade goods. When the girls found a man they wanted to marry he let them go.

Yes, sirree. You can quote me as saying that these early missionaries were pretty tough hombres. And they never once drew a gun on anyone.

The Sewing Circle

WAILBRI WOMEN

CENTRAL AUSTRALIA

←——————————————————————————————————

WE HAVE OUR SEWING circles and our back-yard gossip sessions, too.

This one at Yuendumu settlement on the fringe of the Great Sandy Desert convenes around the water-tap at ten o'clock every morning.

There is nothing much else to do and it's a pleasant way of spending half a day. We bring the babies, and the billycans to make elevenses.

And you should hear some of the talk that goes on! It would make a bullock drover blush.

Most aboriginal people are completely without prudery or reticence in their discussions, particularly in matters relating to sex. Add this freedom of speech to women's natural loquacity and the lack of privacy around communal campfires at night and you may begin to imagine what these tea-parties are like.

The young girls, especially the newly-weds, are the worst of all. If their husbands heard them describing their honeymoon nights in such detail they'd whip them with nulla-nullas.

But we keep our secrets from the men, if only in retribution for their harsh exclusion of us from many of the tribal activities.

There was a time not many years ago when a sewing circle of western Wailbri women would not have yielded one stitch of clothing. We would have been huddled naked behind mulga-wood windbreaks, crouching over smoky fires, covering our babies with sand to protect them from the bitter desert winds.

But look at us now: dresses, sweaters, bonnets, blankets.

And full bellies!

Three times a day we go to a government-run dining room and line up with our children for hot meals prepared by native cooks.

Consider what it was like only twenty years ago: our husbands, the traditional tribal hunters, left us at dawn to stalk wild game in the bush. At dusk they would return, perhaps with a snake or goanna, a wallaby if they had been lucky, empty hands if they were unlucky.

What did we eat in the latter event? We didn't. We stayed hungry until tomorrow or the day after that or until such time as the skill of the human hunters with primitive weapons was more than a match for the natural cunning and superior speed of animals.

The age-old excuse of hunters, 'I caught one but it got away,' had rather a painful significance for us.

Sometimes hunting parties of twenty or thirty men would come home with not so much as a rat between them. We couldn't complain because they had tried . . . and their hunger, after the day's hunt, was worse than ours.

It often happened that a man would have a big kangaroo in his spear sights. He had crawled on his belly for perhaps one hundred yards, moving a few inches at a time. He would then rise behind a tree or a bush and begin fitting his spear to the woomera. In that moment, at almost point blank range, the wind would change. The kangaroo, startled by the human scent, would bound away immediately. Sometimes it happened that a kangaroo was speared but not killed outright; it ran away and could not be found. Or perhaps it would be found weeks later when the flesh was either too rotten to eat, or had been eaten first by the crows and kitehawks.

Believe us when we say that we didn't mind the rain that came once or twice a year to our desert lands. We were wet and miserable because we had no adequate shelter, but at least it meant full bellies. The showers attracted kangaroos from other areas. They congregated around wet ground, knowing that before long there would be green shoots to eat.

Because they were there in greater numbers — and perhaps because that gave them a false sense of security — the human hunters had better luck.

It wasn't a very pleasant experience for a mother of six to watch her empty-handed husband walking back dejectedly to the camp.

'What can we have to eat, Mum?' the kids would ask.

And we would have to tell them, 'Wait until tomorrow. There is nothing tonight.'

'But Mum . . . we're hungry . . .'

That's how it was. That's how it would be now, out here in the desert, if the government hadn't built us a settlement where our kids can acquire rolls of fat and turn on a tap when they want a drink of water.

So praise the government! And pass the leg of mutton!

Left Hand Billy

GUNWINGGU TRIBE

WESTERN ARNHEM LAND

← ───────────────────────────────

In some of the aboriginal tribes in the Northern Territory, every young man reaching his 'majority' must compose the songs to be sung in the ceremonial corroborees at his initiation. They are sung only on that occasion, and then forgotten. One aboriginal composed this song because his initiation came at the height of the flying fox season:

> Look! There are a lot of flying foxes
> Hanging in the tree branches.
> Let us cook and dry some of them in the sun.
> Hit them so they will fall
> Into the mud below the trees.
> Hit them where they are thickest
> And break many wings at once.
> Look out for the crocodile.
> He awaits in the mangroves to catch you.
> Look how the sea-eagle swoops
> To catch them in his claws.
> Listen to the flying foxes call:
> 'Someone is hitting us; we will go.'
> Now we have beaten all the leaves
> And the flying foxes have gone away.

What did I have for dinner last night? Grilled flying fox.

That's my Dad dissecting one after it had been cooked. I'm giving him another to put on the coals. Do I like it? Why, of course. The flying fox is a giant fruit-eating bat. I'll admit there is not much meat on the web-like wings, but the rest is Number One tucker.

We kill them with heavy throwing sticks while they're hanging upside down in trees or caves. I've killed a dozen with one shot — and that's not a fish story.

They fly around our camp at Oenpeli, on the western fringe of Arnhem Land, in hundreds of thousands, especially when the mangoes are ripe. Anybody who couldn't knock down six with one throw wouldn't be trying. It's like an Aunt Sally at a circus, except that this is better fun.

Even white kids could do it, and they're pretty useless when it comes to hunting their own food.

What did I have for lunch? If you must know, my family shared a fourteen-foot python. My piece was about three feet long.

Actually the python almost had one of us — my baby sister Gadjun-wanga. It was like this:

We were all asleep around the campfire — my father, my mother, Gadjie and I. During the night my mother woke up and instinctively felt for the baby.

She wasn't there! Mum yelled for Dad, who jumped up from his blanket and saw the baby's feet disappearing out of the firelit circle.

She was being dragged along on her belly by this enormous python, which had her face clamped firmly in its own jaws, preventing her from crying out.

Dad killed it with a stick, rescued Gadjie, and saved himself half a day's hunting.

But it was just as well Mum woke up when she did.

Sleeping on the ground is all right for Boy Scouts, but I reckon it's time we had a house with proper beds. I've been having nightmares lately.

I suppose pythons are harmless enough. At least they're not venomous like the death adders and the king browns we see around here fairly often. It beats me why so few of our people have died from snake bite.

106

What did I have for breakfast? Well, now you are being inquisitive. You apparently think we eat three meals a day at set times.

The truth is that we eat when we're hungry or when we have food.

But as a matter of fact I did have breakfast today — a piece of crocodile tail.

My uncle speared a big man-eater in the East Alligator River and dragged it home.

There are plenty more where it came from, too. Hence our diffidence about swimming in the river. One never quite knows when a crocodile might decide to have breakfast of blackfeller tail.

What's it like? Frankly, I doubt whether it would ever appear on the menu at the Savoy Grill.

All you can say about crocodile tail is that it's food. Give me grilled flying fox or a piece of bandicoot.

Footnote: Bill Harney's Cook Book gives this recipe for Flying Fox:

'Three or four flying foxes make a good meal. A bush mate of mine said that if he had his way every man would be compelled to eat flying foxes to repletion at least once a year. You saturate yourself with chlorophyll when you eat them, as they themselves eat nothing but honey, the nectar of flowers and fruit.

'Flying fox is food par excellence. No preparation is needed. Just throw them on a fire, burn the wings, and cut the membrane off near the body. When the fire has burned down, put the foxes on the coals, cover them with more hot coals and cook them, entrails and all. . . . When I was in the Gulf of Carpentaria we cooked as many as two or three hundred at a time. They lasted for days. . . . Every part of the flying fox can be eaten except the gall bladder. Even the bones are soft and edible.'

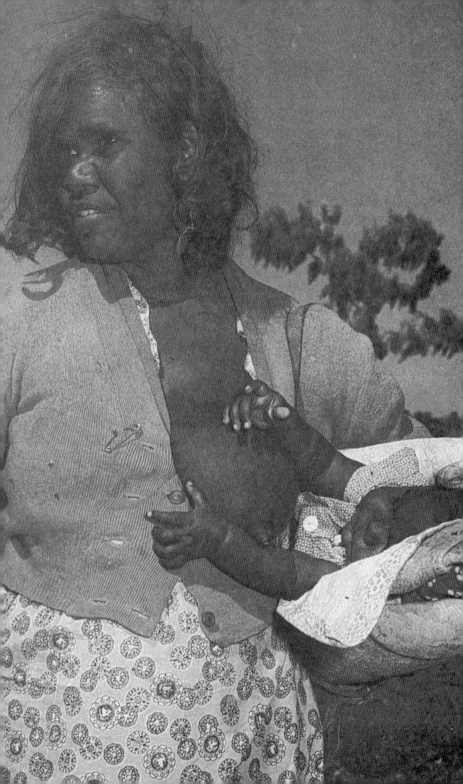

Jean Nagamara

WAILBRI TRIBE

TENNANT CREEK, N.T.

◀——————————————————————————————

THERE ARE NOT MANY mothers in this world who can carry a baby and feed it while walking and yet have both hands free.

My child lies down, completely relaxed, free to suckle until he is full and then sleep or watch the world go by. All this is made possible by a wonderful invention of our ancestors called the coolamon, a light bowl-shaped piece of wood carved from a native tree.

I, Jean Podada Nagamara, wife of Engineer Jack Bind-Naind Jabald-jari of the East Wailbri tribe, placed my son, Baraja, in this coolamon on the day he was born. There he will remain until he is ready to walk. Wherever I go I will carry him with me.

The coolamon is a combined bed, pram, carrying basket, feeding couch and automatic baby-sitter. It can also be used as a dish to carry food, a container for water, or, in an emergency, a shield to protect us from the spears and boomerangs of our enemies.

It beats me why white women don't use them instead of carrying their babies on hips and shoulders.

They could save a lot of time by suckling their young while doing the family shopping. Such a spectacle might cause a bit of a furore on the High Street at first, but when all mothers were doing it nobody would take the slightest notice.

An aboriginal housewife and mother could not operate without her coolamon. If my husband calls me urgently I can go to him with the child at once, ready to move out on a long walkabout.

If the stew boils I can drop the baby on the sand and be sure that neither ants nor spiders will crawl over him for a few minutes.

There is no such tedious task as putting him to bed at night. He is in bed all the time, snug and comfortable and yet able to move freely.

I peel the potatoes while he feeds at my breast.

When my first baby was born Engineer Jack went into the bush and chopped down a coolamon tree. From the light, strong wood he carved three of these carry-alls. He came home proudly, looking like a white father who had just bought his first cot and pram.

'Woman,' he said, 'I hope you will keep them filled.'

All three?

'If it pleases the spirits,' he said.

Unfortunately the spirits have been on a go-slow strike. The best I've been able to do is to keep one coolamon filled.

But Engineer Jack is happy and so am I. We have a concrete house at Warrabri settlement between Tennant Creek and Alice Springs in the Australian heartland.

Jack waters the lawn and grows a few vegetables and drives a motor mower.

When Baraja is old enough he will attend the kindergarten the government has established here on the settlement. Then he will go to the settlement school, perhaps contribute news items to the settlement newspaper, *The Warrabri Corroboree*.

Meanwhile he will remain in the coolamon, attached to my shoulder by a strap when I move, attached to my breast by his mouth when I stop.

Here is a true story about another use for the coolamon:

A few years ago a white man named Jim Stevens was lost in the desert between Warrabri settlement and The Granites. This is the country of the Namma wells — secret, sandcovered waterholes which are so precious that their location is never betrayed.

Our people never camp near these waters. No roads lead to them. Each person going near one must do so by a different route, and all tracks must be erased. We have learnt from bitter experience that to give up a waterhole means giving up our country.

When Jim Stevens became lost, with his canteens empty, he caught a desert aboriginal and chained him to the riding saddle of his camel.

'Ngappa! Water!' he demanded. When the aboriginal refused he had salt rubbed on his tongue, as an aid to developing his own thirst, and then made to walk many miles each day.

At night he was kept chained to the camel's saddle. The white man was convinced that sooner or later he would be led to water. But he didn't know — he couldn't know — that the arrest of the native had been seen by his wife, who followed them all day in the lee of sandhills, and at night crept stealthily to the spot where her husband lay. Quickly she gave him the coolamon she carried and he drank thirstily. In this way he was kept alive for days until the white man perished.

Out in the desert today, beside a Namma well, lie the remains of a camel saddle, and the chain by which a black man had been attached to it. His wife had laboured there, beating the links with stone until they separated and he was free.

Spearman

←─────────────────────────────────────

Upon a rock against the sky I see
A native stand, immobile, poised, alone,
A symbol of the black man — wild and free,
He looks on us, then leaps behind a stone.

ALL I CAN SAY is that I hope no other aboriginal ever sees this photograph. Please don't mention my name or I'll be the laughing stock of every tribe in the Northern Territory.

I must make it perfectly clear that this pose was the photographer's idea. I did my best to dissuade him but he said it 'composed' well and would make a pretty picture.

But I ask you: whoever heard of an aboriginal silhouetting himself against a skyline when hunting? I mean, you might as well send the kangaroo a telegram that a shovel-nose spear is on the way.

It is too long between meals in my part of Central Australia to give the quarry a chance of escape once I'm within spear range.

Getting close enough might take me half a day, depending on the topography. But you can bet that, once there, I would make my throw from behind that big tree rather than from the centre of a pretty frame.

That is the way I was taught to hunt, by the maternal uncle who was responsible for growing me up.

He showed me that a spear was neither a toy nor a photographer's model, but something I had to be able to use well enough to prevent starvation in my family.

My training has continued from before my initiation until the present day. For twelve months I went out with my uncle and learnt first of all the art of tracking. He showed me how to read the stories written in trampled grass and disturbed pebbles. I saw that grass which had been knocked down always pointed in the direction an animal had taken. A pebble dislodged from its bed in the ground was pushed backwards from the line of flight. The track of a snake might be thought to have no beginning and no end; yet I learnt that at each bend the sand was forced towards the tail.

For several years after that I was taught to hunt and kill. My uncle showed me how to camouflage myself with mud, and how to remain hidden behind grass, bushes and trees while approaching my quarry. On the day when I first killed a wallaby my elation knew no bounds, especially when I carried the dead animal back to camp and laid it at the feet of my father.

Now here is a man who wants me to be fully exposed in the very act of throwing a spear! His camera makes a good target!

I make all my own weapons from the mulga wood which grows profusely in this country. The spear shaft is about eight feet long, and the shovel-nose iron tip about twenty inches.

Before the white man brought tin and iron our spears were made entirely of wood, the tips sharpened and hardened so that they would pierce the hide of even the biggest kangaroo.

Then the white man began building the Overland Telegraph line between Adelaide and Darwin. This was a wonderful thing for the tribes.

The iron footplates to the poles were easily excavated from the soft red earth and fashioned with our crude implements into much more efficient shovel-noses.

The glass insulators made excellent cutting tools and horribly jagged tips for some of our killing and ceremonial weapons.

The copper wire was just what we needed for binding the tips to the shafts.

Little wonder, perhaps, that we became the black-haired boys with the Postmaster-General and his line maintenance staffs.

Especially when they discovered that the spear materials they so kindly provided were often found lodged in the bellies of fat cattle driven into the area at enormous cost to feed the linesmen.

Inevitably, there were wars. The worst of these was fought at Barrow Creek repeater station in 1874, two years after the line was completed.

Kaiditj tribesmen came down from the Tabletop Mountains behind the creek and attacked the station.

The officer-in-charge, Stapleton, his assistant, Flint, and six other white men including a linesman named Frank were cut off from the stoutly-walled fortress which was their only refuge. When they tried to regain its safety they were stopped by a volley of spears tipped with O.T. line materials.

Stapleton and Frank were both transfixed and died soon afterwards. The other men reached the station and fired on the Kaiditj, killing a dozen or so on one of the world's loneliest and least-publicized battle-fields.

Make no mistake that an aboriginal hunting spear, in the hands of an expert, is a terrible weapon. The woomera has a tip which fits into a notch at the end of the shaft, thus giving the thrower tremendous 'purchase'. Nothing within thirty yards has much chance of getting out of the way once the weapon is thrown. But the white man has proved that his fire-arms are faster and deadlier. We've never won a battle yet and we've given up trying. Valour is too expensive.

Blackfeller's Dog

KAIDITJ TRIBE

CENTRAL AUSTRALIA

← ─────────────────────────────

WATCH OUT, EVERYBODY! An enemy is approaching.

My dog snarls. My baby whimpers and cries even while she sucks. My own heart beats faster for a White Man is here.

His face is hot. His voice is loud. His tone is cruel.

'Get out!' he says. 'Get rid of that dog or I'll shoot it!' he says. 'Get away from this water — the cattle won't drink while you're here,' he says. 'Go on — *get!*'

Yes, Sir, Master. Where should we go?

'I don't care where you go,' he says, 'as long as you stay away from my water and my land and my cattle.'

My water! Now there's something for you. Whose water was it before you came to this country, Master? This was our water, where the Kaiditj tribe has gathered since The Dreamtime.

My land! Now there's something again. Whose land was it before you arrived, Master? This was our own, our tribal land, taken from us by the likes of you, Mister Hot Face

'I don't care about that,' he says. 'I bought it from the government,' he says. 'That makes it mine,' he says. 'I've got a piece of writing to prove it.'

Ah, yes, he's got a piece of paper. There's no answer to a piece of paper especially if the government stamp is upon it.

Do you know what the answer is if you try to argue with bits of government paper?

117

My people know. They found out . . . the hard way. Policemen. Rifles. Bullets. Hot white faces. Dead blackfellers.

'Niggers and cattle don't mix,' they say.

I saw a piece of paper once. It had been written by a policeman, Mounted-Constable George Montague, soon after mutual killings which happened because some of my people refused to obey the white man and leave a waterhole.

'I cannot conclude this report,' he wrote, 'without paying a high tribute to the Martini-Henri rifle, both as to its accuracy of aim and quickness of action.'

Mounted-Constable Montague and one or two cattlemen who stood behind him had just shot thirty of my tribespeople.

Then they laughed and joked about it in The Mess.

What had my people done to deserve that? It was the time of the big drought. They were desperately hungry so they speared a couple of Mister Hot Face's cattle and ate them. They drank some of the water the squatters said had to be left for the cattle.

For this they were shot dead. That has often been the penalty when a black man has defied a white man.

Some writers didn't see anything wrong with the way we were treated.

Mrs. Dominic Daly wrote in 1887: 'Would that one could write the record of this year without having to include the usual tale of aboriginal outrage and murder . . . the experience of years shows that they are not amenable to civilisation . . . the annals of 1886 teem with the murders of white men . . . many punitive parties have been sent out to teach the niggers a lesson . . . we are learning that summary justice is not only most effective but most humane. Twenty murders of white men have been reported this year. *It is not known how many natives were killed.*'

Alfred Searcy's *In Australian Tropics* also contains some interesting white-feller views on human life: 'Mostly the niggers bring the trouble on themselves by interfering with cattle. Reports seldom reach the police. I know of one case in which a whole camp of niggers was wiped out. I got a letter from a man who was attacked by niggers in the Gulf country, and had eleven spear wounds. In his letter he said, 'I now shoot on sight; have killed thirty-seven to date.' Another man told me he never carried a revolver. He said he inflicted all his punishment with a stockwhip and a wirecracker. When he wants to be particularly severe he cuts the top off a sapling, sharpens the remaining stump, and drives it through the palms of both hands of the nigger. He assures me that he is ceasing to have trouble with the niggers.'

Do you blame us, now, when we shrink from any white man who comes around? Do you wonder that the hackles rise on the neck of a blackfeller's dog?

Are you surprised that my child quakes, afraid that the visitor means to harm her?

White Man, thy name is Fear.

Walkabout

←————————————————————————

THE URGE TO TRAVEL is strong in the breast of every aboriginal whether he is a nomad or a sophisticated townie.

We have the original itchy feet.

The Nabobs of Tourism haven't yet realized the potential fortunes to be made in exploiting our weakness.

Ships and aeroplanes, cars and trucks, roads and railways pass us by. Therefore we walk and we walk and we walk and we walk . . . and we sit down. Then we walk and we walk and we walk . . . and we sit down. We might go on for a week or a month or for three months, depending only on the availability of game and water . . . and, of course, the travel weariness.

We are two men of the Loritja tribe, Frankie and Johnnie. At dawn this day we said to our wives, 'We go walkabout. You come behind.'

We left at once, waiting only long enough to gather our spears and boomerangs — for they are all that we carry.

The women, laden with swags, cooking pots, billycans and piccaninnies, are always a mile or so behind. At dusk we will have to wait for them to catch up so they can cook the game we have caught. We will guide them to us with signalling smoke.

You think we should do a little more of the heavy carrying?

Listen, Mister, that's a white-feller habit.

If you want to tote your wife's bags and pick-a-back her piccaninnies when she's tired that is your business entirely.

But please don't try to reform us.

Aboriginal women are traditionally the tribal beasts of burden.

You must remember that our people have lived for centuries on the game we hunted.

We would have died out long ago if our hunters had been burdened with impedimenta they had to put down before being free to throw a spear at a nervous kangaroo.

That's why you see aboriginal women buckling at the knees under loads big enough for a drayhorse.

It is the law: the man hunts, the woman carries.

Perhaps this is one explanation of why our women never appear as keen as white women to travel and broaden their minds.

They're inclined to regard it as anything but a holiday.

We get a great laugh from watching white men staggering under their loads while their women carry nothing more than a handbag.

What's wrong with some of these fur-coated ladies humping their own blueys? And perhaps balancing a hatbox on the head as our women carry swags?

We have no maps, no roads and no paths to guide us.

The sun is our only compass, marking the way with shadows which point us home.

There are no hotels along our walkabout trail, no air conditioning, no h. and c., no b. and b.

Our bed will be scooped in the sand at the place we have reached when the sun sets.

If we are lucky we will have a kangaroo or some lizards and snakes to cook over a fire we will kindle with firesticks.

It is scarcely a honeymoon suite — but this is the way we have always spent our holidays.

We don't grieve about luxuries we have never known.

And the price is right.

In spite of our great urge to travel, however, we seldom leave our tribal country. Most of us never do. Few of us ever will. We have many thousands of square miles of our own to explore, so why should we want to go elsewhere. Our northern neighbours, the Aranda and the Wailbri, stay in their own backyards, too. Occasionally we meet on neutral ground for inter-tribal parleys by the Elders. But the average tribesman has no desire to go away from home.

What is there to see in Wailbri country that we haven't got here? The same kangaroos and wallabies, the same snakes and lizards, the same mulga, and the same red soil. Perhaps the mountain ranges vary, but scenery has never impressed us. You can't eat it. A range is beautiful to us only for the game it hides. We wouldn't give you two shillings for the Blue Mountains or the Swiss Alps unless it could be proved that the kangaroos there were fat and plentiful.

In any case, our totems are here with us. This is where our ritual places are. This is where our symbolic corroborees are performed. This is where our young men are 'made'. Our religion is indissolubly bound to our country. So that if we leave it for a holiday elsewhere we leave our religion behind . . . and our totems. There are no pagan pagodas in the big cities where we can celebrate our rituals. Therefore we will remain here until, like our waters and our land, the tribal religions are also taken from us.

Donald Jabaldjari

ANMATJIRA TRIBE

CENTRAL AUSTRALIA

◄──────────────────────────────────

I'M DELIGHTED TO meet you.

My name is Donald Campbell Jabaldjari of the Anmatjira tribe.

I live at Mt. Allan cattle station, way out west of Alice Springs, where I'm a stockman and horsebreaker.

You won't mind if I appear to boast?

Diddy Smith, the white man who employs me, says that I can ride anything on four legs.

Frankly he is right.

Young colts that throw other good buckjumpers never throw me. It might take a long time to get into the saddle on a fresh colt, but once there I get off when I decide.

I don't take dictation from any horse yet foaled.

Diddy pays me thirty shillings on every colt I break in for him.

Let's see if I earn my keep:

First round up the young colts and yard them. That might take any-thing from an hour to half a day.

Cut one out of the mob into a yard on his own — a circular yard so that he can't get his head into a corner and his heels rampant.

Hobble his forefeet.

Get a bridle on his head, a bit in his mouth, and a saddle on his back.

All this time, of course, the horse will be trying to murder me, rearing up on his hindlegs and attempting to poleaxe me with his forefeet. He'll

125

be screaming and grunting his objections and often rolling in the dirt because of the unaccustomed hobbles.

Make sure the girth is tight. In a few moments I'm going to need all the security I can get. I ease my weight on to the near side stirrup iron, relaxing, and repeating the process a few times until the horse gets used to the idea.

Then I hold my body low as I slide across the horse's back and lower myself into the saddle.

Let go! Open the gate! Hang on!

I'm now in for a few frantic minutes of expert bucking by a highly indignant young colt which has never before been insulted in this fashion.

He snorts, rears backwards, rears forwards, bucks gamely and jarringly in a futile effort to dislodge me and the saddle.

But he's got no chance. I've done this before.

I pull hard on the rein, keeping him going around in the same direction until he begins to tire.

Then I give him a little of his own medicine: a couple of slaps with the reins and a tickle along his flanks with my spurs. Get him used to the idea that this is what happens when he misbehaves.

In ten minutes, foam flecked and frightened, he stands quietly in the yard. I pat him gently with my hand, the treatment to be expected in future when he is good. He'll catch on.

In a few days I'll have him eating out of my hand.

Maybe The Boss will ride him on the coming cattle muster. Soon he will be a valuable stockhorse, enjoying the gallop after wild bullocks, herding them instinctively without assistance from the rider.

Some of the other stockmen here reckon that my idea of a broken-in horse varies considerably from theirs. They say that because Donald Campbell thinks a colt is quiet and rideable doesn't mean that others can ride it.

But I don't know what they're complaining about. When I've finished with a colt he is like a rocking horse.

Breaking in the colts, of course, is only a part of my duties at Mt. Allan. I am one of those people — the black stockmen — of whom it is said that the pastoral industry would collapse without them.

I think there is truth in that; frankly I can't imagine that many white men would put up with the conditions and the wages offered to some of my tribesmen, especially in the Kimberleys.

I am well cared for. I get a decent wage which is paid 'cash-along-finger'. I have decent living quarters. But you should see some of the pig-stys up north. Most of them are built of bits of old bark, hessian and tin.

There is no privacy. Entire families cook their meals on open fires, which means they are limited to grilling meat in the coals.

I can hear the bosses saying, 'They wouldn't understand anything better.' Perhaps that is true enough, because they've never been given the chance.

Tea is made in salvaged milk tins. A bully-beef tin becomes a pannikin. Knives and forks? Fingers were made before knives and forks. A bath? 'Ah, they're dirty people,' I can hear the bosses again. 'They wouldn't know what to do with a bath. Let 'em wash in the billabongs.'

It is surprising, therefore, that so many of my people were faithful to the stations for so long.

One reason was that they soon became addicted to tobacco. The station store was the only place they could get it. Food and tobacco often represented the major part of a stockman's wages. He worked or starved — because he had forgotten how to hunt.

Today things are very different. The Welfare Branch has insisted on minimum standards of accommodation and a minimum wage. And not before time; many of my friends were on what is known as the Damper Line, which is 'way below the Bread Line.

Old Wally

WAILBRI TRIBE

CENTRAL AUSTRALIA

←———————————————————————

SHORT-BACK-AND-SIDES, if you don't mind.

I may even try one of those new-fashioned rinses. I'm a little tired of the red and yellow ochre and the white clay we've been using as hair dyes for centuries. Perhaps a little purple, or a nice blue for a change.

And this style? Isn't there something that can be done about it? Perhaps an urchin cut would suit me. I've had this style since I was a boy. The same old thing, year in and year out: thick coils matted with wax and dust and grease from my eating fingers. (Well, a man has to wipe his hands on *something* after a meal!)

In all my life my hair has never once been washed, not because I have dirty habits but simply because we have never had enough water for such luxuries.

I thought you might like the honour of being the first to wash it for me.

Then we could have a shampoo, a face massage, manicure, and pedicure. I've never worn boots, so those old feet of mine will be rough. You'd better sharpen your scissors.

And watch what you're doing with that razor! I've got enough cuts on my back, shoulders and chest without wanting others around my face and neck.

Those on my shoulders are sorry-cuts I inflicted myself to make me sad when my wife died. They certainly did.

My back is covered with scars from cuts made by men who were cross with me. Confidentially, I was a bit of a Romeo in my youth, but I never

129

once managed to take a woman away from her husband without him finding out. Hence the cuts.

The curved marks on my chest are tribal cicatrices I was given during my initiation as a young man. After the wounds had been made they were filled with ashes in order to form the decorative pattern you see.

We were pretty tough in those days. Considering that the incision was generally made with a sharpened piece of iron, stone or wood, and the ashes came from a polluted campfire, it's remarkable that so few of us died.

Why was it done? Because it was the tribal law. It was a kind of trial by ordeal we had to suffer stoically before qualifying as men.

Anyway, what's so strange about skin decoration? Thousands of white men have tattooed arms, legs, backs and faces. Women pierce their ears and suspend pendants from them. They wear stones around their necks, rings on their fingers, and bracelets made of bits of iron and other minerals.

Well now, Mister Antoine, what about this haircut? I'm ready when you are. But no long-winded yarns. I'm not interested in horse racing, dog racing, football, or even the weather.

I'm afraid our women don't take much interest in their appearances. Few of them are likely to get their photographs in *Vogue*.

And yet a Melbourne hair-stylist, Mr. Rene Henri, recently showed what can be done for aboriginal women if they like to take a little trouble.

Mr. Henri was at a camp on the wild western border of Arnhem Land. He was shocked by the scraggy and matted hair of the women, and regarded it as a challenge to his artistry.

He selected two of them, Nancy Aljurudj and Daphne Jarlgud, and gave them expensive bouffant hair styles.

First of all he took them to a billabong and watched while they shampooed their hair twice. Then he sat each of them in turn on an upturned drum and went to work.

When he had finished? 'Ah, we had two pretty girls,' he said.

Mr. Henri says that aboriginal women have beautiful hair that is fine, wavy, shiny and 'worth its weight in gold.'

He was so impressed by his own handiwork that he said there should be a beautician in every aboriginal camp, mission and settlement. Perhaps he is right. Perhaps a bouffant hair style would do more for the assimilation and sophistication of our women than a year in school. Let us face it: the appearance of many of them is tragic. It bars them from close contact with the rest of the community.

I'm thinking of getting a red, white and blue barber's pole and setting up a business. The Wailbri Women's Salon.

These women have no money, so I'd have to take my fee in goannas and snakes.

I could always give change in witchetty grubs.

Mischief

PINTUBI TRIBE

CENTRAL AUSTRALIA

← ─────────────────────────────

Whitefeller man he make me wild,
Singing out, singing out, 'Stop that child!
'Him yell too much and it hurt my ear.'
Then I make answer, 'Listen here,

'One-time you were little-bit kid,
'Do just same as 'nother one did,
'Have good time and make man wild,
'Now you old you cry "Stop child!"

'My young lad, him good-feller boy,
'Play in mud with stick for toy,
'Then when happy you all-time growl,
' "Stop that kid . . . him too much howl."

'Cat and puppy-dog play all day,
'Piccaninny all-about learn that way;
'Listen, Boss, him not dumb calf,
'So let kid laugh if he want to laugh.'

MY NAME IS MISCHIEF. I wonder why.

The white man who took my picture said I had a mischievous face. He said to my mother, 'I'll bet Mischief is always in mischief.'

My mother said, 'His name is really Jacob, but everyone calls him Mischief. His third name is Trouble. He's never out of it.'

'What does he do?' the white man asked.

My mother said, 'To start with, if you don't get out of the way quickly you'll have that toy spear thrown in your chest.

'Last night he put a goanna in my swag and a handful of multi-pronged bindy-eyes in his father's.

'His father sat on them as he got into bed. The entire handful stuck into his backside like steel filings to a magnet. I thought it was a great joke and was laughing as I crawled down under my blanket.

'Then I felt a goanna move near my feet. Next moment it shot up between my legs, over my body, and out past my head, slapping me with its great tail as it scuttled away. I was terrified. Mischief was huddled down under his blanket, heaving with mirth. But he changed his tune when his father took to him with the flat side of a boomerang.'

'Is that all?' the white man asked.

'Oh, goodness no!' my mother said. 'He does something like that every day.

'Yesterday he tied the tails of two dogs together. Then he let them go. You've never heard such bedlam!

'One of his favourite tricks is to put a billy of fat on the fire in place of a billy of water. Eventually someone makes tea with the boiling fat and Mischief watches while we take a mouthful. It's not only terrible; it also lifts the skin off your tongue.

'When the hunters are out he just loves to hide behind a tree with a dead snake or goanna on a string. He waits for one of them to pounce, then quickly withdraws the string. Professional hunters who are supposed to be able to see whether a snake is dead or alive detest the derision which always follows, for Mischief spreads the story very quickly indeed.

'He has learnt how to make perfect wallaby tracks and to lay a false trail. His father once followed a wallaby for two hours, before discovering that the trail led back to camp — and Mischief. He couldn't say anything about that; in fact I think he was secretly pleased at the boy's ability, especially when he got complaints from other hunters.

'At the mission school he has often been in trouble for crawling up to the teacher's desk and tying his shoelaces together. You can imagine what happens when the teacher stands up.

'I'm sure I don't know what we are going to do with him.

'He won't comb his hair or wash behind his ears or use his handkerchief. He never cleans his teeth — and yet they're like pearls. Mister, what am I to do?'

The man said, 'Give him a good spanking.'

My mother said, 'He has one every day without fail.'

You know, Mister, I could tell them what to do. They should just let me be as I am and enjoy it all as good honest fun. The trouble with grown-up blackfellers these days is that they're becoming as serious as white men. They're losing the ability to laugh.

Ha! How d'ya like that, Mister?

Got ya fair in the belly!

Charcoal

MALAK MALAK TRIBE

DALY RIVER, N.T.

←————————————————————————————————→

YOU'LL LAUGH WHEN you hear my name: it's Charcoal.

Mumma-belong-me — ooh, dear, I beg your pardon, Sister Carmen — I mean my mother calls me Charcoal because I'm as black as midnight.

Another boy here is named Midnight. That's because he is as black as charcoal.

Me belong Malak Malak tribe alonga Daly River — I'm sorry, Sister Carmen. What I mean is that I belong to the Malak Malak tribe at Daly River. Some people call us the Mulluck Mullucks, especially when they want to throw mud at us.

This is very good country here on The Daly. The river is full of barramundi and crocodiles and sharks and other good tucker, I mean food.

We are water people. My ancestors were using canoes for generations before the white man came. That is one reason why our skins are so black and we look so well fed.

We have more food than we need, and often more water, too. When the big floods come we have to run along quick time — I mean quickly — for the high ground.

I remember one year when the mission station was under water. All the goats were drowned and carried downstream. Snakes were floating around in the convent. Hundreds of kangaroos were drowned. They were washed off islands and carried out to sea.

That was a scary time. We had to go in canoes to a big hill where we were safe from the rising water. But when we got there we found we had company — a couple of big wild buffaloes. And more snakes. And thousands of scorpions and centipedes. And pigs. Oh, yes! We saved our pigs by taking them in our canoes to the high ground.

We have good reason to love the Sisters here. They saved us during the flood, but there must have been times when they were very frightened. They not only had snakes in the convent, but bush rats, too. And dozens of frogs perched in rows around the walls. They spent one night on the convent roof with the aboriginal girls. We went on to the presbytery roof with Brother Abbott. But these roofs sloped sharply. The Sisters couldn't go to sleep because they feared the girls would fall into the water. Once they did hear a loud 'Plop', and thought it was a girl fallen off, but it was only a baby kangaroo the children had brought with them. We could see big fish swimming around the houses.

When we were going to the hill in the dinghy we paddled around the tops of trees. On the hill our tents collapsed in the wind and the rain. The Sisters slept between us and the water to protect us. Thirty children were packed tight in one shelter while the cyclone raged. We were there for a fortnight. What a time that was! Ever since, I have tried to be helpful to the Sisters.

Sister Carmen has been teaching me how to count, and to read and write in English, and to speak correctly.

She hates me to use pidgin.

One day during the wet season a big storm was brewing. I went to the door of the schoolroom and was leaning against it when the first crack of thunder came.

I turned to Sister Carmen and said, 'Properly big feller rain bin come up.'

For a whole month after that I had to say to Sister six times every day, 'The rain in Spain falls mainly in the plain.'

In spite of these petty irritations it's a good life. We have our own small canoes and at week-ends we can race up and down the river as much as we like.

We also have tiny fish spears, just like Dad's, with which to catch barramundi.

Sometimes we stay out all night, canoeing and playing along the river and its banks, always keeping a weather-eye cocked so that the big fish — the crocodiles — don't catch us.

I'm a Catholic like Sister Carmen.

We're all Catholics here at the mission, only some of us are more Catholic than others.

Yes, I go to church. Yes, I say my Hail Marys. Yes, I go to Confession. . . . Hey, now look here Mister, what would a boy like me have to confess?

Oh, yeah . . . yes . . . there was that time Midnight and I sneaked into the kitchen and took some bread and jam.

Oh yes, and that time Sister heard me swearing. 'The bloody thing,' I said. More than that, too.

I had heard a white man talking. He used a lot of new words. Next day I said them to Sister. I thought she would be very pleased with me. Instead, she covered her face and ran away.

Ah, well . . . Marmuk.

You thought I was swearing in the dialect, didn't you?

No. Just a farewell. 'I'll be seeing you.'

Mininderri Corroboree

ARANDA TRIBE

ALICE SPRINGS

←————————————————————————————————

THERE IS NOTHING NEW under the sun, especially when it comes to secret societies. We had them for generations before the white man came. There's no Freemasons' Lodge, no Order of Oddfellows, no Antediluvian Buffaloes, no Elks, no F.B.I. or Ku Klux Klan that we didn't think of first – with some rather important variations, of course.

For instance, we don't drag white men out of bed just before dawn and have them swinging from a tree as the sun rises. We don't vilify or debar people because of race, religion or colour. But we have almost everything else, right down to secret signs, secret handshakes, secret knocks, and a gibberish that is just as incomprehensible as some that is spoken in what you probably regard as more civilized fraternities.

We have our equivalents for your Knights of the Garter, your Knights Grand Cheese, Grand Masters, Grand Wardens and Worshipful Brothers.

And we have initiation ceremonies which we'll wager very few white men would submit to.

A young initiate of the Aranda tribe near Alice Springs lies on top of a fire for a few minutes to teach him courage and a proper sense of stoical self-restraint. Dozens of tribes practice circumcision as an initiation rite.

But, of course, we have never known anaesthetics nor, until recent years, did we have such a civilized surgical tool as a discarded kitchen knife.

Perhaps it isn't surprising, therefore, that our youths who are 'made' in this fashion and passed through its tortures without whimpering can truly be said to have become men.

The Gubabuingu tribe at Millingimbi, on the north coast of Arnhem Land, tests a youth's readiness for manhood by knocking out a central upper tooth. He has his tooth prepared for extraction by a tribesman who cuts the surrounding gum with a sharp stick to loosen it. There are no dental surgeons where they live and this is far from a pain-killing injection.

The tooth is then knocked out in a way which, if practised by modern dentists, would double the amount of horror and dread already to be found in their surgeries.

A piece of wood is placed in the initiate's mouth. He bites on this to keep his open jaw steady. His head is held firmly by the dental nurse, generally one of the strongest men in the tribe. The surgeon then knocks out the tooth with a wooden chisel and hammer.

The idea is not to cry out. No tribesman who is worth his salt would want to betray that he has suffered excruciating pain.

The initiates of the Alawa tribe, on the Roper River, submit to a two-year period of enforced silence with certain relatives. This is an exercise in self-control.

They also submit to indignities which would horrify most white boys. One of these is that the initiate must sleep on a blanket beside his sister-in-law and her relatives, but not speak to them. They are all naked. The women may talk to him but he cannot answer, except by nodding his head. They bring him food and drink, and eventually decorate his body for the ceremony in which he is circumcised.

Apart from the ban on speech, a young Alawa initiate is put under a lifetime prohibition on eating certain foods and a temporary taboo on others. These are generally associated with his totem.

While his wound is healing he is forbidden to swim in any river, billabong or creek. He may talk to other boys, but if a man approaches he must be silent. Above all, he must avoid speech with the dancers who performed at his initiation, and with his mother-in-law. There are those who would say that the latter would not be a hardship.

Perhaps this speech-taboo explains much of the reticence of the aborigines. A man who is half-dumb for two years is seldom garrulous thereafter. There are other tribes whose people would benefit from similar interdictions, and they're not all black.

Having passed through these ordeals a young man is considered fit to face the most rugged physical tests that life may be preparing for him.

That is why, today, you never hear an aboriginal groaning or crying out when he is physically distressed.

Our young initiates know that they have withstood greater pain than any they are likely to suffer in the course of a normal life.

This knowledge gives them strength.

They are men indeed.

Billy and Albert

WAILBRI TRIBE

TENNANT CREEK, N.T.

◄─────────────────────────────────

IS THAT A HUNTING dog, a water dog, a pet dog, a racing dog, a cattle dog, or just plain dingo?

It could be a bit of all these, but you'd never guess what we really use it for — it's a bed-warming dog.

Out in the Wailbri desert where we have lived for generations there has often been a shortage of firewood, especially after a tribe has camped in one area for any length of time.

So we use our dogs to keep us warm on winter nights.

We've heard white people talking about sleeping under six blankets.

Out here in the desert where blankets are scarce a man has to use his dogs instead.

If you hear an aboriginal talking about a Six Dog Night you'll know that he means it was very cold indeed and six dogs were needed to keep him warm.

What about the fleas? The first forty years are the worst. After that you don't notice them nearly as much. Actually we wouldn't be surprised if some of the dogs complained about the human fleas they get from us.

Of course, our dogs have uses other than as bed-warmers.

They help to hunt our food when we're old and slow. In drought years in the desert they sometimes *are* our food. Ever tried grilled greyhound?

And they always provide good moving target practice for white men armed with rifles.

There is nothing a station owner likes better than to spend his day 'shooting blackfeller's mongrels.'

And we've generally got to be in fair physical trim to dodge the bullets ourselves.

If you've wondered why our dogs generally race away with tails between their legs at sight of a white man it's simply that they're being discreet.

We've never yet known one of them that didn't cringe when The Boss appears.

We are Billy Jagamara and Albert Jungarai, both of the Wailbri tribe.

We live at the Warrabri aboriginal settlement near Tennant Creek in Central Australia.

What is an aboriginal settlement like? Ours is one of the biggest in Australia, with a population of 520. Water (always our first priority) comes from underground, miraculously pumped to the surface by the clever engines of the white man.

Not only are engines used for water. They bring us light, too, and refrigeration.

We have a school, a hospital, a dining hall and kitchen, a training centre, a garage and workshop, about a dozen houses for the staff, groups of aluminium and concrete houses for the aboriginal residents and — most importantly — a co-operative store. One of our own people, Ted Plummer, is on the board of directors. The store sells everything we need.

Our children are being educated here. Our young men are learning trades. Our young women are studying the domestic sciences.

It has cost the government a lot of money to build this settlement — more than a quarter of a million pounds — and there are several others like it in the Northern Territory. Some of our people still live in primitive conditions. There aren't enough houses for us all. Many of us have lived in the open for so long that we wouldn't want to be in a house. But there are others who do, and we must say they're looking after them well. Old Engineer Jack, for instance, tends his garden and waters his lawn every day. His example is being followed by younger married men.

146

The word 'Warrabri' is derived from the Warramunga and Wailbri tribes. Once, way back in The Dreamtime, we were enemies. The white man was our enemy, too.

They were our tribesmen who opposed the bearded Scot, John MacDouall Stuart, when he first attempted to ride from south to north across the continent in 1860 — only about thirty years before we were born.

He and his men killed a lot of our people with rifles when they began throwing spears.

It was the first time the Warramungas and the Wailbris had experienced this invisible death — but once was enough.

When Stuart returned the following year they let him through: in fact, they gave him a wide berth.

Before that we had some fine old wars with the Warramungas.

But now we don't fight anybody. We leave it all to civilized white men. And the dogs.

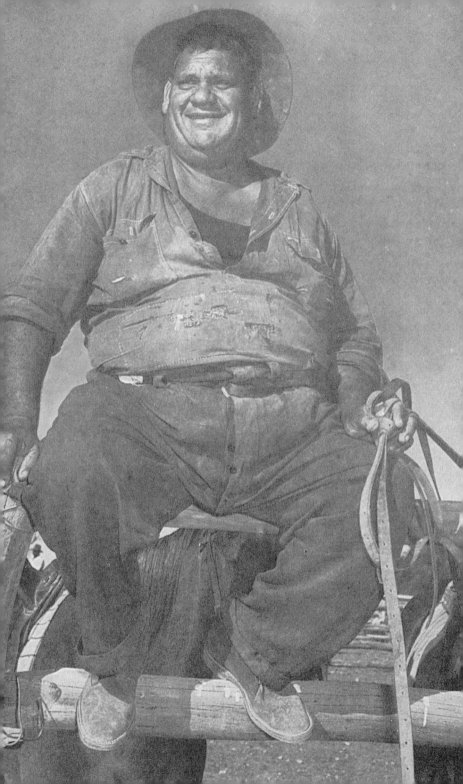

Pompey

PART-ABORIGINAL

NEWCASTLE WATERS, N.T.

←——————————————————————————————————

REDUCING PILLS WERE MY downfall.

I was once an active stockman, a good rider, an asset to any mustering camp in the Australian Never-Never.

My base is Newcastle Waters station, midway between Darwin and Alice Springs, where I was born fifty years ago.

The trouble is that Newcastle Waters raises some of the fattest and juiciest beef in the entire Northern Territory.

I have always eaten several pounds a day — fried, roasted, grilled, boiled, corned — with lots of potatoes and damper or bread.

Before I knew what was happening I had become an addict. I was taking Newcastle Waters beef almost as though it was a drug.

And, like heroin or opium, it left its marks on my physique.

The horses were first to complain. Good colts which had never hesitated to carry me through a full day's mustering were exhausted by midday. They developed sore backs and had to be put out to grass.

In my country there are few mirrors and fewer sets of bathroom scales, so I really didn't understand that I was a changed man until old Oscar Shank, at the local store, said there was no such thing as a bigger size in trousers than those I was wearing

My shirts were Triple XOS.

One day in Tennant Creek The Boss put me on a weighbridge.

'Three hundredweight and a bit,' the attendant said, as though he was

149

weighing a fat steer. 'If you want it in human figures I'd say twenty-two stone or three hundred and eight pounds.'

Then and there I decided it was time Pompey Allum took himself in hand.

I went back to Newcastle Waters with all the resolve of a remorseful alcoholic or a chain smoker. I was determined to beat my terrible addiction to food.

That night the Boss wrote away for a supply of reducing pills. When they arrived I began my long battle against the insidious poison I was consuming.

Alas! I loved them. They were like lollies and I ate them by the bagful.

And they made me ravenously hungry.

So this is a Before-and-After photograph. My present weight, after the reducing course, is roughly three hundredweight. The Boss won't let me ride the horse. He says I could give it a ride.

You've been thinking all this time that I'm an aboriginal, but you're wrong.

I'm what a few people call a halfcaste white. Others would say I'm a halfcaste aboriginal. I'm both.

There are those who call me Yeller-Feller. They are not my friends.

There are several thousand half-caste people in the Northern Territory. The white settlers came north in the 'sixties and 'seventies, battling from Queensland across the Kimberleys and north from South Australia into the gibber plains and the dormant heart.

Some were the descendants of peers. A few were criminals. They were average men absconding from the law or their wives, or selectors coming out to build their crude homesteads in the never-never.

They had hard lives. They were tormented by heat and dust, flies and the shortage of water. They faced droughts and floods, heartbreak and disease, isolation and danger.

There were no white women in the country to soften their mood or their beds, or comfort their bodies. It was no place for them, and so the trials of celibacy were added to their other suffering.

Some remained pure for as long as six months, but eventually most of them realized that black women, who could be bought for tobacco, were better than none. Trade was undoubtedly done.

Half-caste children were born and grew up on the stations and settlements. More often than not, they lived in the blacks' camps, in sight of the superior homesteads where they were conceived. Many of them were acknowledged by their fathers, who gave them a name if little else.

For half a century we were ranked by the whites with the blacks. But now all that has changed. We have citizenship automatically. We live in good homes in white communities in all the towns of the Territory. We are paid award wages and margins for skill. Except for the colour of our skins, we are equal in all respects with the white men.

I am more equal than most — because there is more of me.

What does a halfcaste stockman do on a cattle station when he's too heavy to ride?

The Boss has been good to me. Perhaps too good. For many years now I've been the station gardener and butcher.

I've got a half-acre plot of ground and plenty of water to raise vegetables for the kitchen — and for Pompey.

I slaughter the station beef and prepare it for the meathouse, whence it goes to the cook for the dining room table — and for Pompey.

My cross stays with me. No matter what happens I can never escape from some association with food.

The thought of it makes me hungry . . . here, hurry up with that photo . . . that's the dinner bell!

151

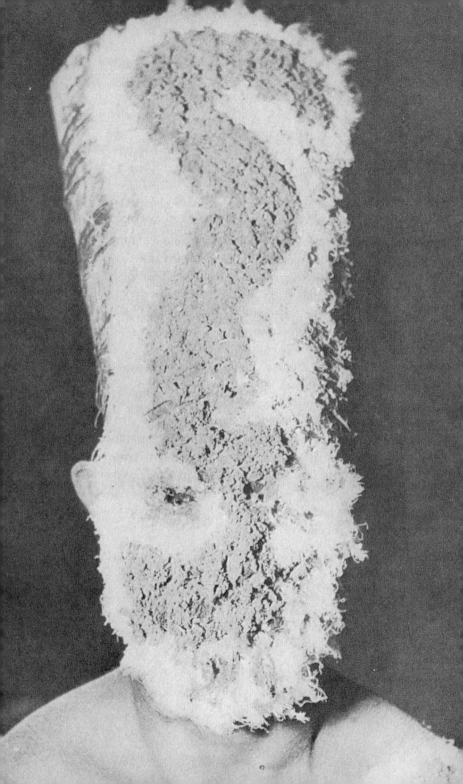

Kadaitcha Man

PITJENTJARRA TRIBE

CENTRAL AUSTRALIA

I AM THE All-Seeing-Eye. They call me Kurakajarra of the Kuniai totem. The Rainbow Serpent you see on my head-dress is the symbol of God, the Giver of Life who brings water to the earth. I am also the mythical Kadaitcha Man who strikes down the evil and unbelievers in the tribe.

There was a time when I kept order among our youths. We had no bodgies, no widgies, no Teddy Boys. At my command the young men were taken from the women's campfires and given the facts of life by The Elders. There was no molly-coddling with us. We taught them the hard way, with initiations, with trials by ordeal, with ritualism which scarified and purified any who might be straying towards juvenile delinquency.

I am also the tribal executioner, ritually appointed to legally break the neck of any man who might betray one of our secrets. The white man's law is powerless before me. It takes its retribution, of course, but it does not abrogate my power. Most tribesmen would burn rather than reveal a secret of The Elders. Nevertheless, betrayals are not unknown.

It is then that I wear my feathered Kadaitcha boots, sneak silently upon my victim while he sleeps, break his neck with one blow, and creep away in magic boots which leave no tracks.

Selly was one who was found with his neck broken. His was a political killing like them all. He made the mistake of talking openly to girls about those things he had pledged never to mention. The other young men had to be shown that such behaviour would not be tolerated. So Selly died.

But a broken neck is a difficult matter to explain to a white doctor,

153

especially as Selly was discovered in bed. The white Medicine Men say that broken necks just don't happen in bed.

And so one of our tribesmen was arrested. His name was Charlie. The police took him to Alice Springs and the Big-Feller Judge sent him to gaol.

But Charlie, even if he had been the Kadaitcha Man, had no option. He had to obey the tribal instruction to kill. Not to have done so would have caused his own death at once.

The Roper River tribes have a Mulunguwa who is roughly equivalent to the Kadaitcha Man. He, too, is tribally appointed to murder a transgressor — perhaps a man who has speared a bird while it sat in a tree that had been made Taboo, or taken wild honey from a similar tree.

The Mulunguwa (the name means "The One Alone") leaves the tribe and goes into the bush to live by stealth, perhaps for as long as a year. He never camps in the same place twice and is never seen by other tribesmen. Rather than leave evidence of his whereabouts by making a fire he eats all his food raw and drinks nothing but cold water. He stays on gravel ridges where his tracks will not be easily seen. He carries nothing but his spear.

He lives alone — and waits . . . waits for the inevitable day when the man he has been ordered to murder will walk away from the camp and enter the bush. That man has then not long to live . . . he does not hear the Mulunguwa, whose bushcraft has been developed to an uncanny degree. And if he hears the gentle 'swish' as an iron spearhead cleaves the air it will be too late. Before he can turn the spear will have struck him between the shoulder blades, and pierced his heart. He is dead almost before he hits the ground. The Mulunguwa removes his spear, obliterates all his tracks, and moves away as quietly as before. Nor does he return immediately to the tribe. The dead man's body has to be found. There has to be a period of mourning. He must remain absent long enough so that suspicion does not fall on him. When he thinks that the coast is clear he will go back to his family . . . as though returning from a long walkabout . . . and hope that accusing fingers will not be pointed at him by the bereaved relatives.

This man has done nothing more than kill as he was ordered to by the tribe.

Is it right, therefore, that our legally appointed executioner should be sent to a white man's gaol?

Albert Pierrepont broke more necks than any other hangman but there was never any suggestion that he might be gaoled for doing so. In fact the government paid him to do it.

Then why must our hangman suffer a penalty?

Interference by your government has weakened the authority of The Elders. It was a sorry day for our influence when the first preachers came here and said 'Thou shalt not kill'! It was still a blacker day when the Government Man came and said, 'If you do we'll put you in gaol or execute you.'

Because the birth of black bodgies and the advent of juvenile delinquency among our tribespeople dates from the very time of these edicts.

The white man told us about his laws.

But he didn't tell us what moral right he had to force them upon us, an independent people who owed him nothing. Nor did he suggest any means other than our own harsh rules by which we could keep order in the tribe.

The result is that we break a white law every time we observe a black one.

Yet I — the Kadaitcha Man — am still part of the pattern of our tribal lives.

I will remain so — *Sine Die*.

Ambrose

TIKALARU TRIBE

BATHURST ISLAND, N.T.

←————————————————————————————————

My name and address? Certainly. It is Ambrose Lilangpungarimi Tipung-wuti of the Red Ochre group of the Tikalaru tribe at Bathurst Island, Northern Territory of Australia.

My Dad and Mum call me Ambrose for short and frankly I don't blame them.

Mum's name is Joan Marakampitimau of the Ironwood group of the Munupi tribe. Got that?

Do you want to hear Dad's? I thought not. I just call 'em Mum and Dad, so I don't see why you can't do the same.

Some of the tribal names we've got here are no joke at all, especially for a feller who stutters.

How would you like to live in a family of six with names like Waring-nalla Ampriwauaningia, Tipulampuralatjimiri, Ipilingpurrulalwula, Tipa-liakitau Apipiamarrila, Kitjaminaualungawi Pukamyalui, and Nguluun-gayi Nguluungayimmi?

I wonder how they expect a kid like me to say Good Morning to them all. By the time I get through they're waiting for me to say Good Night.

And you should hear the priests trying to pronounce them, here at the Catholic mission station. Now they've hit on the idea of renaming every-one to make it possible for young fellers like me to find their way around.

But some of the names they've chosen are almost as bad: Annunciata, Concepta, Mary Magdalen, Francis Xavier, Pius, Aloysius, Anastasia, Chrysostom, Dionysius.

Do you think that sounds like a Catholic mission? There are others: Paul, Peter, Simeon, Ruth, Margaret Mary, Matthew, Mark, Luke and John.

On the Lutheran Mission at Hermannsburg in Central Australia many of the aborigines have German names: Henoch, Johannes, Hedwig, Gottlieb, Reinhold, Rudolf, Anton and Emil.

The Church of England missions are full of Toms, Dicks and Harrys. It is sometimes possible to place an aboriginal's country by his white-feller name.

It won't be long now before I start attending the new school. Mum and Dad reckon they're going to make a Little Gentleman out of me, whatever that means.

I'm to learn how to speak correctly, and how to read and write and count.

But I can count already.

Listen: Little mob, little bit big feller mob, big feller mob, properly big feller mob.

I've got to learn to wash behind my ears and how to use a handkerchief.

Cissy stuff, I reckon.

I'd much rather be out with the boys spearing a few fish and wallabies.

Ever eaten grilled wallaby? It's terrific. Always remember to peel the fur off first. Otherwise it tastes like a charred overcoat.

Do you think my Mum and Dad are handsome? I do. Mum has lovely crinkly hair which is exclusive to the coastal aborigines. Our skin is like burnished copper, a kind of golden black which reflects light.

The physique of aboriginal people is strongly influenced by their proximity to the sea.

One of the commonest phrases of the tourists who travel to Central Australia and then on to Darwin is: 'The natives are so different here that you'd never know they were the same people.'

That is true. It is also understandable, because we never have any shortage of food . . . fat food. The desert people not only are short of food, but what they find is lean.

We're always laughing, except when a photographer calls. We laugh because here on Bathurst Island we are insulated from the worries of the world.

International politics, wars and threats of war, glut and famine, boom and bust all pass us by.

We live on a South Seas island of plenty. The sun — and our gods — smile upon us. Our bellies are full, our hearts are light.

We live for each other in The Land of No Work. The Forty-Hour Week doesn't exist. It's the No-Hour Week — unless you count hunting as work. But we regard that as play.

Come up and join us sometime.

Corroboree

TIWI TRIBE

MELVILLE ISLAND, N.T.

THE IMAGINARY BAMBOO clan of an imaginary tribe of aborigines may have had a tribal song, part of which may have been:

> The campfire dimmed . . . then came our own show,
> Off went the shoes and the radio;
> Off went the clothes of the whitefeller man
> And a clan stepped out in the tribal plan.
>
> The Gods were calling in the dust and heat,
> The grey earth lifted from the broad splayed feet;
> They danced and pranced till the wise Moon-man
> Said, 'Back to the earth for the Bamboo clan.
>
> 'The Gods of the mountains and Gods of the plain
> 'Give all the tucker and send all the rain;
> 'The whitefeller's law is for whitefeller man,
> 'But we black men run to the tribal plan.'
>
> The Song-man chanted as he gave the song,
> Swaying were the Elders, stamping in a throng;
> Boomerangs rattled to the thud of feet
> As the dancers quivered to the tapstick's beat.

There is nothing new under the sun.

Elvis Presley reckons he invented rock-'n'-roll. Someone else invented the twist.

Listen, our people have been rocking and rolling, swinging and twisting for centuries.

We have a different name for it, a word common to many aboriginal dialects: Corroboree.

Some of these modern dances are poor imitations of parts of our corroborees.

The Wargites at Delissaville, the Tikalaru at Bathurst Island, the Ngulkpun at Mainoru, the Malak Malak at Daly River, the Anula at Booroloola: these are all tribesmen who could teach Presley something about Rock.

We've got Barefooted Rock, which is more than he ever had.

We'd like to see him on a hot day, stripped naked with us, beating out the rock on the hard ground, raising the dust, bare feet bleeding unknowingly, not only the pelvis but the whole body swaying to the rhythm of beating sticks and didgeredoo.

He has a drum to give him the beat. But could he pummel the earth with his foot so that it reverberates like a drum? We do.

Could he chant the song cycles that go on for hundreds, some of them for thousands of verses, for as long as six months, all telling the stories our ancestors were told by their ancestors?

Could Elvis, as we do, insist that his tribal women should not watch certain dances?

Could he make his women perform other dances with their heads and eyes lowered, never meeting the eyes of the wild men around them?

Could he, after a night of corroboree, lie back in the sand and eat a haunch of grilled kangaroo? Or a goanna? Perhaps a snake? A stew made of witchetty grubs?

And chew pituri which has been rolled in ashes? Or smoke nikki-nikki in a crab-claw pipe?

We think not. Elvis makes a meaningless noise. Our corroborees are ceremonials steeped in centuries of tradition.

Through them we beseech our pagan gods, expiate our sins, honour

our fathers, remember our dead, placate our enemies, and invoke the food-spirits as white men do at their harvest festivals.

We paint our bodies at corroboree time and daub ourselves with clay and feathers.

What's so funny about that? Have you ever seen a painted white bride in her finery — in a dress reserved for just that occasion? Red paint on her lips, blue paint on her eyelids, black paint on her eyebrows, and many colours of paint on fingernails and toenails. They use powder as we use the talc we pound from the chalk cliffs and the clay deposits. They wear lucky charms and carry horseshoes.

There is just this difference: it is the male aborigines, like male birds, who are adorned and preen themselves. Our females, like female birds, remain drab and unadorned.

Nature intended it thus.

Mary Armina

WORORA TRIBE

NORTH-WEST AUSTRALIA

←——————————————————

MY NAME IS MARY ARMINA. I'm from the Worora tribe at Kunmunya mission station, Port George IV, Kimberley region, North-West Australia.

A jolly good place to be from. The weather is impossible. Every summer seems a year long, with the temperature staying around one hundred and ten degrees for weeks and months.

Do you wonder that I seldom wear more clothes than you see me in now?

Then the winter comes and the nights are cold, so I bury myself in the sand — right up to the neck.

That way I am not only snug; I also have protection from the quiet-footed two-legged wolves who come sneaking around when the fires are low.

Gerta Kleist, who made this sketch, said I looked ineffably sad. That's because my husband died recently. The marks on my arms are sorry-cuts for him. I cried out very loud when they were made, like a good wife should. The sincerity of a woman's mourning wail is helped immeasurably by cuts like these inflicted with a not-too-sharp implement.

But my appearance of sadness is not only for my husband. It is hereditary: something that has been handed down to me through many generations of hardship, suffering, and the awful knowledge of my people that, until recently, they were a disappearing, unwanted race.

You've heard the terrible stories of how the tribes were hunted and shot at, just as though they were wild game. Those stories are true.

The squatters were right, of course, when they said that cattle didn't like mixing with niggers.

Many of my people were forced to live in exile in the places the white men didn't want. They died like flies. Those who protested or were defiant were shot down like they shoot our dogs today.

'Real cheeky niggers,' the white men called them.

A real cheeky nigger was one who didn't agree with The Boss, or wanted to stay on tribal ground that had been taken over for cattle.

My grandfather told me stories I'll never forget. Stories about crucifixions. Stories about mass drownings. Stories about men who were thrown to crocodiles so that their bodies would never be found.

'A crocodile eats the bones, too,' the white men said. 'There is never a corpse to be identified.'

The dead men weren't all black. But when a white man died it was generally because he had taken a black woman away from the tribe.

Our people have never raised any objection to the drovers, cattlemen, station hands, miners and itinerants having 'gins', as long as they were not abducted.

It was the taking away of our women that caused so many white men to be speared. We know that we were invaluable to the early squatters. Quite apart from offering sex freely in a land too harsh for white women, many of us became splendid horsewomen. We led men to water, settled the mustering camps, boiled the billy, and tracked the horses each morning.

As Alfred Searcy wrote, 'It is not possible to over-emphasize the advantages of having a good gin in the outback.'

Cattle stations, in fact, were founded by black gins, as we are called. One of them is Beetaloo, near Newcastle Waters. Old Bulwaddie Bates settled that station when his fullblood wife, Nora, led him to Briggs lagoon. It was virgin country, inhabited only by wild natives. They resented the intrusion and often tried to kill him. At night he placed a decoy swag near his shack, but took good care to sleep in another several hundred yards away. The decoy was regularly pierced by spears.

Nora Bates, of the Djingali tribe, had a big family of half-caste children, who now run the station. She lives there still, old and blind, but loved and cared for. Her son, Watty, remembers her carrying the family's water on a yoke across her shoulders. The nearest post office in those days was at Camooweal, five hundred miles away. Their goods came from Oodnadatta by camel train. She dressed her sons in flour-bag shirts and her daughters in flour-bag dresses. She remembers the cruelties, and one special time when three hundred aboriginal men were driven into the nearby McArthur River and shot at a spot where there were plenty of crocodiles.

All that has ended now and my people are multiplying again. But do you wonder that I look forlorn?

However, I must snap out of it. I must try to forget the past and live in the future.

Maybe one of these nights I'll find a nice young wolf has called, one who would make me want to crawl up out of the sand to him.

My vital statistics? I'm not too sure, but I know this: A fifty-pound flour bag fits me perfectly.

Billy Motogari

WAILBRI TRIBE

TENNANT CREEK, N.T.

←————————————————————————

MY NAME IS BILLY MOTOGARI of the Wailbri tribe. I have lived in the desert near Tennant Creek all my life. I am seventy-five years old. I have never used toothpaste or brushed my teeth since the day I was born. I still have a complete set. I have never suffered from toothache, abscess of the gums, gingivitis or pink-toothbrush.

The dentist came to visit us at Warrabri settlement and he said to me, 'Billy, you've got wonderful teeth for an old man. How do you clean them?'

I told him. With my tongue.

Maybe once a month when I was younger I rubbed them over with sand on the tip of my finger, but I haven't done that for fifty years.

Of course they're not as sharp as they used to be. A lifetime of bush tucker has worn them flat like a cow's.

But these days I eat white man's tucker. You don't need good teeth for that.

The dentist was complaining here the other day that the teeth of aboriginal children were beginning to decay. He made several extractions and many fillings.

'Why is that, Billy?' he asked.

I told him straight. It's the dreadful soft tucker they eat. Do you know that there are kids at this settlement who have never tasted snake, goanna or wallaby?

I ask 'em: What did you have for dinner today?

'Stew,' they say. 'Bread and butter puddin'.'

Then they go off to brush their teeth with paste out of a tube!

Is it surprising that they wake up during the night and cry with toothache, just like white kids?

Another thing about white man's food: Since they began eating these horrible stews and puddings my people have acquired many new ailments. One is called appendicitis which was unknown in the tribe when we lived in the bush on tucker we hunted ourselves.

We have acquired other worse diseases simply by associating with white men.

His bequests to us include tuberculosis, syphillis, leprosy and the common cold, from which hundreds of my people have died.

Perhaps it is not quite right to say that the white man brought us leprosy. That was probably introduced by the Malayan traders who came to the north coast long before Europeans, and then by the Chinese who came in as indentured laborers to build the Pine Creek railway They stayed to mine gold. But they left behind a country polluted with one of the worst diseases known to mankind. Even today, the Pine Creek district is heavily endemic with leprosy.

Fortunately it has not spread south of Newcastle Waters in the centre of The Territory. This, at least, is one of the blessings of living in the desert. The people who suffered most when leprosy struck were the aborigines. One or two white people and a few halfcastes were affected. The great majority were fullblood aborigines. That almost certainly happened because we lived in the kind of dirt and squalor in which the disease flourishes, and with the kind of long and intimate contact that is said to be necessary for its transmission.

Of the more than two hundred patients in East Arm leprosarium near Darwin today, less than a dozen are aborigines. They are taken from their tribal country, away from their husbands and wives, their children and their relatives, and put in a place where they have the best of care and attention — but are miserable nevertheless because they are not only away from home but banished altogether from society. They have been "Unclean, Unclean" since Biblical times.

One of the greatest levellers of all has been German measles. Two hundred tribesmen perished in a single epidemic a few years ago. We had no immunity and therefore no resistance to it. Once infected, the victims died as though touched by the plague.

Alcoholism and drug-addiction, particularly to narcotics, are other benefits which the great white civilization has handed down to us.

There is no such person as an aboriginal who doesn't smoke, and that includes the kids. And if he gets the taste of grog he is an alcoholic for the rest of his life.

Don't think I'm preaching. I like a drop myself and I couldn't live without tobacco.

What I am saying is that the aboriginal race would be better off if the white man had never come to Australia. We have been kept on the fringes of your society, absorbing its evils but denied many of its benefits.

Quarter of a million of my people have been killed off in the process.

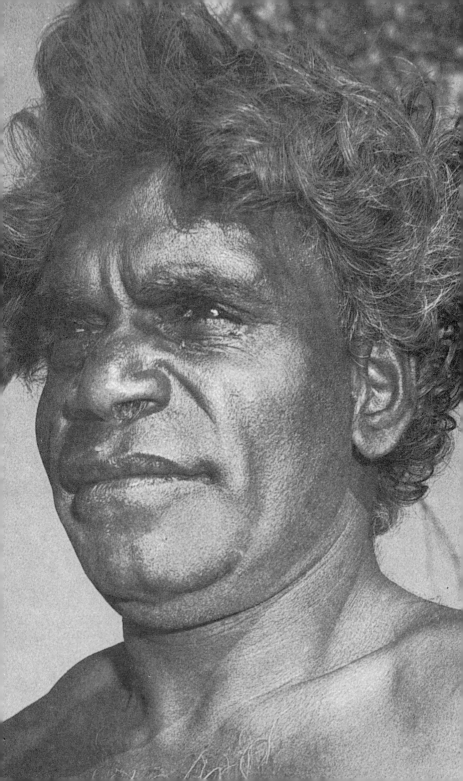

Johnny Jambadjimba

WAILBRI TRIBE

CENTRAL AUSTRALIA

←————————————————————————————

I'm what I appear to be: The Boss.

Nobody in the Jambadjimba clan of the Wailbri tribe tells Johnny what to do. I give the orders around here, without 'please' and 'thank you.'

It's not that I'm deliberately rude. Our language simply does not contain such words. There is no need for them in a society in which every person's duties are clearly defined.

'Please' and 'Thank you' are the words which our children are finding it most difficult to absorb in the education they are now being given in the schools.

They have no trouble learning and pronouncing them, but they cannot understand why anyone who is entitled to give an order should say 'Please', or why 'Thank you' is politer than a grunt.

The lesson of good manners by the white man's standards is one of the first the teachers try to impress on our children. They often have trouble in reconciling one code of behaviour to the other.

Some of them think our children are mannerless louts who should be cuffed into an acceptance of the politer forms.

But let me say that we consider certain normal acts of white people to be quite barbarous.

For instance, you seldom see two aborigines shaking hands. The risk of defilement is great enough without that kind of encouragement. You

173

never know what another man might have been doing with his hands. Yet white men shake almost every time they meet.

And this habit of kissing, whether in public or private, is an obscenity.

An aboriginal man never kisses his wife or anyone else. Frankly we think it is unclean. What we say about the passionate kisses served up for our edification by film stars wouldn't flatter them if they overheard.

I've noticed that white men wait for their women to pass first through a door. They rise when a woman enters a room, give them seats in public transport while they stand, carry their parcels, beg their pardons, and get down on their knees to propose marriage.

How humiliating!

These things would be unthinkable to any of my tribesmen.

When I enter my campfire circle my wives rise and slink into the background until summoned.

On walkabout they carry my swag, my food, my water, and my children. When they run out of hands they use their heads.

There are no beg-your-pardons.

As for proposing marriage, the woman knows to whom she belongs from earliest childhood. She goes to him at puberty. Whether she likes him or not has probably never occurred to her.

But of all the undignified faults of white men I think the worst is his habit of arguing with women and allowing them to join in his conversations with other men.

Wailbri women are seen and not heard in the company of men.

I don't know of any tribesman who has ever been influenced in his actions by anything a woman might have said. But white men's thrones have toppled on a woman's whim.

You keep your emancipation and your equality. You're welcome to them. I'll remember to say 'Please' and 'Thank you' when I'm given food or tobacco. It is a small price to pay.

However, I sometimes wonder how much longer the male aboriginal will be supreme in the tribes.

There are disturbing signs that the women are being obsessed with what, in another society, might have been classified as dangerous thoughts. There are even more disturbing signs that the young men are beginning to accept back-chat from the young women, and even defer to them.

This is all being caused by education. If we were the teachers the pupils would be told quite clearly that man was paramount and woman a mere chattel.

But we are not the teachers. They are white men, and often white women! And the kind of influence they are having on our children can well be imagined.

Every aboriginal child of school age on the settlement here at Yuendumu is attending classes. Their very first lesson concerns their personal hygiene — they are taught to wash regularly, and that is foreign to their natures. But once they are in the mould it isn't long before they accept that other habits should be discarded and replaced by refinements. And so, I fear, boys who now scramble past girls at the school door will soon be standing back and saying, 'After you, my dear.'

That is going to be a sad day for tribesmen like me. I'm wondering what my reaction will be when a woman first says to me, 'You should not interrupt so rudely when I'm speaking.'

It could well be that her flow of impeccable English will be cut short by a nulla-nulla on the head.

Brown Eyes

WARGITE TRIBE

DARWIN, N.T.

←———————————————————————————

W<small>HY IS IT THAT</small> all good things, especially food, come in awkward parcels that take hours to unwrap?

I think it amounts to nothing less than cruelty to hungry children.

An hour ago I climbed a coconut palm and came down with this beauty. Ever since then I've been slowly dying of starvation while trying to get through the hairy fibre.

The trouble is that my mouth waters uncontrollably, wetting the straw and making it more resistant to my fine teeth.

In a crisis of this nature there is much to be said for the white man's eating tools. (A Darwin magistrate said recently that any aboriginal who ate with a knife and fork was a civilized man, and I think he was about right.) I could make good use just now of a carving knife or a machete.

Instead, I'm condemned to at least another hour of impatient tugging before I get through to the sweet milk and the crunchy nut.

Imagine the howls of a white boy who was given a toffee wrapped like this . . . like one of those mystery parcels they have at parties.

But with us such misfortune is the rule rather than the exception. It's little wonder we eat our food raw or only half-cooked — when we finally get through to the edible part the exercise has made us ravenous.

Let's examine a few of our natural foods: Kangaroos and wallabies are wrapped in thick fur. Snakes and lizards have tough skins. The hide of wild buffalo is used for industrial belting. And every inch of a crocodile is encased in a horny leather that is much prized for women's footwear and handbags. Our spears bounce off the shells of turtles. The females bury their eggs deep in sand. And natural fruit comes to us like this — whether it's coconut, pandanus nut, or fibrous yam.

The god responsible for such matters has been at great pains to ensure that our salivary ducts are kept in good working order.

On the other hand, of course, we have a number of advantages that are envied by white boys and girls.

Foremost of these is the complete absence of those parental phrases we've heard so many times coming out the windows of their homes:

'Have you washed your face and hands and done behind your ears?'

'Have you cleaned your teeth?'

'Have you cut your fingernails?'

'Keep your arms and hands off the table!'

'Don't put too much in your mouth!'

'Don't talk with your mouth full!'

Aboriginal boys are in the happy position of never having to wash, clean their teeth, cut their fingernails, or to learn 'manners'. (At least, that used to be so; at some of the mission stations and settlements these things are now beginning to catch up with us.)

Nor do we have to worry about keeping our clothes clean and not playing in the dirt.

A boy who has no clothes is not concerned with the dust and the mud that might adhere to his skin — it will all blow off or wear off in time.

But do you wonder that the Australian aborigines have the strongest teeth in the world?

Who needs a toothbrush when this kind of alternative is put to work daily.

It makes you wonder about toothpaste, and this latest craze for fluoridation of water.

What the human race needs is less soft tucker, and more sinewy meat to chew.

I've no doubt that goanna tail would be better for modern youth than the hamburgers and icecreams they eat.

My elder brother goes to school here at the mission. On his first day he was given a tooth brush and told that he must use it three times daily.

And I must say he does use it three times a day — but to keep his fingernails clean. His teeth don't need it.

Incidentally, hacking one's way through the rough shell of a coconut is really only half the torture.

Before we can begin this process we first have to find a coconut. They are generally at the top of palms thirty or forty feet tall. We have no ladders.

It is possible to wait until a coconut falls. That might be today or next week. We haven't the patience to sit there and hope.

We therefore have to climb the tree, without the aid of ropes or spikes. And, before you fall, remember that there is no safety net at the bottom.

Don't you blame me, therefore, if I appear to be greedy.

Gambling School

WARGITE TRIBE

DARWIN, N.T.

←————————————————————————————————————

I'VE WON TWO NEW wives in this game but I've just seen them and I'm not sure whether they should be counted as profit or loss.

Anyway, I'm doing my best to lose them again — with the unintentional help of my partner, who persists in trumping all my aces.

I am Tommy Imamul of the Wargite tribe near Darwin. That's me smoking the photographer's cigarette. (He thought he would be allowed to take the picture for nothing.)

My mates are Snider Gurdaj, Nipper Yetba and Jimmy Two.

Jimmy Two, unfortunately, is my partner. What he doesn't know about this game is considerable.

I suppose you could say that a lot of money changes hands at places like Flemington, Royal Ascot, Kentucky Downs, Longchamps and a few other racetracks. But I doubt if the people who go there are more inveterate gamblers than the aborigines.

We are never happier than when squatting on the ground anywhere in the bush playing cards endlessly for money, clothes, tobacco and, occasionally, wives. Gambling is like a drug to us. Once we have acquired the habit we are addicts forever.

Our favourite game is called Sevens. You wouldn't understand the rules even if I explained them in detail. I will say this: they are flexible enough to allow barefaced cheating by the influential. Important tribesmen can deal off the bottom of the deck and get away with it. Unimportant tribesmen wouldn't try.

In this respect the game is a little one-sided. I've never yet known an influential man to lose. Like the rich, they get richer as the play proceeds. The amazing part about all this is that the losers don't seem to mind.

They regard losing as part of the black man's burden.

I wouldn't know about that because, if you don't mind me being immodest, I am a man with some influence myself.

White men have sometimes been unwise enough to sit in on one of our games.

The last one escaped with his trousers — but little else. He hasn't been near us since. Maybe he cannot yet afford to replenish his wardrobe.

In these sophisticated days, however, we normally play for plain old money.

And in this regard we have another laugh over the white man. Let a policeman catch him gambling at cards or even having an off-the-course bet on a race and he has some heavy explaining ahead of him.

But we are not citizens and therefore cannot be made answerable to laws except those in the criminal code. We do pretty much as we like.

There is generally enough money in several gambling rings here at Bagot settlement to make any gaming squad detective turn grey.

Mind you, we have a rather more liberal code of ethics than white gamblers. A man who is 'fleeced' can borrow from the winners and not be expected to remember the debt. That is often a most convenient arrangement for the losers and it can be expensive for the winners.

Playing cards is something we have acquired from the white society. But long before the arrival of Captain Cook and the first settlers we had our own camp games. Hide and Seek was one of them. So was Hunting the Object, although we had to vary it to suit our environment. A smooth circle was made on a sandy patch of ground. An object about the size of a pinhead was hidden, with just a fraction of it showing above the sand. Then the players were called in to find it — but they must not scratch the surface. Even the minutest object was soon found by men and boys whose eyes had been trained to studying tracks.

Hunting and Guessing was another of our games. A man returning from the hunt hid his catch and asked his relatives to guess what it was. The winner was given a choice piece of the kill as a prize.

Bowling the Boomerang was our equivalent of the white boy's bowling a motor tyre, except that it was obviously much more difficult to keep a boomerang on the move.

And we had ball games before balls were brought to Australia. Our balls were made of grass, tied with vines, and covered with bees-wax. The ball was kicked into the air and, once started, could not be touched by hand. The idea was to keep it in the air with the feet only – an accomplishment much more difficult than playing soccer.

Now, of course, aboriginal men and boys are ball-fiends. They play Australian Rules football, rugby, basketball, baseball, water polo – any of the contact sports. They are not interested in tennis, golf or cricket.

Bruno

ARANDA TRIBE

ALICE SPRINGS

←————————————————————————————————————

MY DEAR GREAT-GRANDSON,

It is not often that your old ancestor writes a letter. To be truthful, this is my first attempt and I am being helped by Douglas Lockwood. He has a writing machine that is a mystery to me. I see his fingers flying and the keys hitting paper where they leave incomprehensible marks.

He says he is putting my ideas into print that you will understand because you are now at school and able to read and write. I have told him to say how much I envy the aboriginal children today with the knowledge of a language other than our crude dialect and for their ability to read and write and count and express abstract thoughts.

Why, when I was a boy . . .

As you can see, that was a long time ago. I lived with my people in the desert west of Alice Springs. Our home was a mulga windbreak in the red-brown sand.

When I was a boy we lived off the land, eating the food we could catch by stealth or fleetness of foot. It was often a long time between meals. . . .

When I was a boy our waterholes were so scarce that they were secret. We called them 'Jilla', which means that they gave us life. In the western tribes there was often no separate words for 'camp' and 'water' — they meant the same thing so we used the one word.

When I was a boy I slept on the ground with neither a blanket nor a pillow. When the winter cold came I covered myself with sand to keep warm.

When I was a boy we had no education at all. I learnt the Aranda dialect by listening to my people speaking it around the campfires. No conscious effort to teach me was made by my parents or anyone else. My vocabulary was limited to two or three hundred words. I could make myself understood by my tribespeople about the things that mattered — food, water, life and death. I could say 'sun' or 'rain', but never express an opinion that it was a nice day or a wretched day.

I wish I could say, like many white men, that when I was a boy I had to walk three miles to school. But I cannot. I have grown old and tired as a primitive man, burdened with thoughts that I have been unable to transmit because my tongue has been tied with the knots of ignorance.

I have seen you, my great-grandson, laughing, playing, learning and talking with the children of your generation. I have heard unintelligible sounds and my heart has rejoiced because I have always known that only by absorbing the white man's culture, by learning as he learns, and by competing with him on his own level . . . only in this way may our people be truly assimilated and come at last to win respect and recognition.

'There was a time when I disbelieved that any of our people could acquire the highly technical skills of the white man. I argued that it couldn't be. And yet today, in Alice Springs and Darwin, there are many tribesmen and women doing skilled and semi-skilled work.

'Ted Cooper drives a bus for the Northern Territory Administration. Phillip Roberts is a medical assistant with the Department of Health. He goes out alone into the wilds of Arnhem Land to make his own diagnoses and treat his people with pills and injections. His brother, Jacob, is training to be a missionary. Holder Adams is a plant operator with the Department of Works. Davis Daniels is a hospital orderly, and so are several others. His brother, Dennis Daniels, is a patrol officer in the Department of Welfare.

'When I was a boy it was said that black people could never live in white men's houses, but only in bark humpies or behind brush shelters.

186

Now many of our people are not only living in white men's houses, but in white men's suburbs — integrated peacefully in the community around them, without any suggestion of racial conflict of the kind we have seen in America. Would you believe it . . . they seem to be welcome!

'You wonder why it was such a joy to me to see you playing football with white boys. When you grow up you will understand. It wasn't always so. I can remember when we were not allowed to play any sport with or against white people. But now all that is changed. We play *against* them at football and basketball and water polo, and we play *with* them in the same teams. This is a wonderful source of pride to your old great-grandfather.

So listen well, my boy, when the teacher teaches. I know it is difficult for children whose recent ancestors were hunters to settle down to sedentary life. The call of the wild will be strong in your heart all your days . . . and perhaps in your children's hearts.

But then it will disappear and they will be train drivers and teachers and parsons and writers and maybe even fly the aeroplanes across our tribal lands.

Remember what you learn. Absorb it all. Keep it with you so that you might impart it to your own children as our tribesmen handed down to me the ability to hunt, to track animals, to smell water, to throw spears and boomerangs, to dance corroborees . . .

Bush Boys

LORITJA TRIBE

CENTRAL AUSTRALIA

←——————————————————————

OUT HERE AT Angas Downs station, 150 miles south-west of Alice Springs, life was always lonely and monotonous. We were Children of the Sun, naked as the changeless blue sky, anonymous, friendless, wilderness waifs who were never likely to get their photographs in print.

But look at us now. We've both got shirts and shorts and big balloons. And The Boss here says he wants to put us in a book, whatever that might be.

Life changed for us recently when tourist companies began to exploit a lump of rock we have out this way.

Actually it's quite a big rock. In fact we are told it is the biggest single rock in the world.

The white people call it Ayers Rock, but to us and our Elders in the Loritja tribe it has always been Uluru. More than five miles around it at the base. Twelve hundred feet high. A huge monolith where our ancestors danced interminable corroborees with tribesmen who came from hundreds of miles away.

Many spirit people still live there: the serpent people, the mice women, the kangaroo-rat men. It is a sacred place because of its importance as a living symbol of the things and the times that are dead.

Although The Rock is a sacred place it has never been secret or taboo. There are dozens of legends and myths concerning its origins. The geologists say that it was originally laid down as horizontal sandstone. Its present tilted position was caused by upheavals in Protozoic times when the great Central Australian fault-planes occurred and formed the folding now apparent in the mountain ranges around Alice Springs.

That's what *they* say. But we know better. We know it was formed in The Dreamtime by our own culture heroes. And those big round holes in the cliff-face. Why, surely everyone knows they were made by the spears of warriors who were attacking an enemy camped there.

We also know that a big aboriginal woman named Bularri lives inside the rock. Oh, yes, we know it is solid; nevertheless, she lives inside. Ask any of our tribesmen.

Among the enormous boulders at the base of The Rock there is one with a hole in it. This was made when it was pierced by a heavy spear — because the boulder at that time was being held aloft as a shield by an opposing tribesman.

Mutidjula rock-hole is important to us, because it was on this part of Uluru that the sacred serpent lived. The serpent saved the lives of thirsty people in times of drought; it was lured from its hiding place by cries of Kuka . . . Kuka . . . Kuka. As it came out it disgorged hundreds of gallons of water which flowed down to the perishing people below.

Now the tourists come in droves — four thousand of them in six months of this season.

Most of them are women. They leave Alice Springs before dawn in a big bus and drive through the mulga for three hundred miles before reaching Uluru after dark.

On the way they pass through Angas Downs. That's why we're wearing shirts, even if they are a size or so too large.

Our drab and monotonous lives have changed miraculously. They give us lollies and toys and balloons (we're just waiting for them to go so we can prick them on a spinifex bush) and they all take photographs.

In four years we estimate that we have posed at least ten thousand times. We think that next year we might charge professional models' fees.

And, oh, the questions! You'd never believe it.

'What's your name, sonny?'

'Do you live here?'

'Do you like it?'

'How old are you? Do you go to school? Do you have plenty to eat?'

One day when the bus came in we submitted as usual, but then decided to ask a few questions ourselves. We said to a middle-aged lady, 'What's your name, Missus?'

'Where do you live?'

'Do you like it there?'

'How old are you?'

'Do you go to school?'

'Do you have plenty to eat?'

She was very cross and said to her friends, 'What cheeky children!'

But why is it cheeky for us to ask these questions and polite for her to do so?

What *are* our names? Look, Mister, if you don't mind we'd prefer to remain anonymous. It's enough to have our privacy invaded like this, and to be photographed and questioned and prodded and patted on the head without getting our names in print.

Our Lady of the Aborigines

FROM THE PAINTING BY

KAREL KUPKA

◄──────────────────────────────────

Now THE BIRTH OF Jesus Christ was on this wise: When as his mother Mary was espoused to Joseph, before they came together, she was found with child of the Holy Ghost.

Then Joseph her husband, being a just man, and not wishing to make her a public example, was minded to put her away privily.

But while he thought on these things, behold, the angel of the Lord appeared unto him in a dream, saying, Joseph, thou son of David, fear not to take unto thee Mary thy wife: for that which is conceived in her is of the Holy Ghost.

And she shall bring forth a son, and thou shalt call his name Jesus: for he shall save his people from their sins.

Then Joseph, being raised from sleep, did as the angel of the Lord had bidden him, and took unto him his wife.

And knew her not till she had brought forth her first born son: and he called his name Jesus.

     *   *   *   **

Ah! So you thought that Mary was a white woman.

How can that be when you see her here as she is, Our Lady of the Aborigines?

You thought that Jesus was a white man?

How can that be when you see him here as the Holy Child, black as the heart of Herod?

It is not the colour of a man's skin that matters, saith the Lord.

It is the colour of his heart.

For if the heart is white the pigmentation is neutral in the eye of the beholder.

We have been a little disappointed that angels are always shown as white as snow and devils are black like us. In no picture book ever printed have we seen a black angel or a white devil, and yet we know they exist.

The tormentors, defilers and slanderers in the private hell of the entire aboriginal race are invariably white.

The missionaries came to the tribes to purge our paganism, to save our souls, and to anoint our wounded bodies. There are few aborigines today who do not confess that most of them were remarkable people who lived only to convert us from our heathen ways and to embrace their Christ.

Of course, we had our own beliefs. They were pagan, certainly, but none-the-less fervent, and for many years the men of God had a tough time convincing anyone that theirs was the right way. Bishop Francis Xavier Gsell discovered that at Bathurst Island. On the day he retired, after forty-six years among us, he admitted that not one aboriginal was a true Christian. There were some who professed Christianity for the rewards it brought them . . . the rice-Christians. That position is changing slowly.

The work of the missionaries should not be written off as wasted just because they failed in their primary task. In many places our people had great need of physical help. We needed medicine, and proper food, and in the early days only the missionaries were there to give us these things. If for no other reason, they will never be forgotten for that . . . the men like Bishop Gsell and Father McGrath, the men like Stanley Port and H. E. Warren, the men like T. Strehlow and F. W. Albrecht, who went into remote areas and still ministered to our bodies when they found that our hearts did not gladly accept the new religion.

They established clinics and hospitals and . . . perhaps just as importantly . . . they opened schools where some of us learned to read and write long before the government showed an interest in such matters.

It seemed that they lacked only one thing: the ability to explain why black men should embrace a white God.

What reason could we have to believe that Our Saviour belonged to a different race from our own?

They exhorted and cajoled and induced us into the ways of righteousness.

But there were many Doubting Thomases among us.

Now all that has changed.

It took a European artist, Karel Kupka, to show us the Holy Mother and Child as we have believed them to be.

See how the Holy Child sits in typical native fashion on the Mother's shoulders, one leg draped around her neck, a hand resting fondly on her head.

This is a natural pose adopted by piccaninnies.

Woven into the background are reproductions of symbolic native art taken from ceremonial spears, carved corroboree poles and sacred churingas.

Doesn't it give you a sense of nobility, and of the natural dignity that characterizes natives who are not degraded by a corrupt environment?

Our Lady of the Aborigines will hang in Darwin's new Catholic Cathedral, there for all to see that a lowly, humble piccaninny, a child of the bush, a child of nature, has been born of a Virgin Mary.

Girls' School

TIWI TRIBE

BATHURST ISLAND, N.T.

◀─────────────────────────────────────

HERE AT BATHURST ISLAND where the shade temperature is around one hundred degrees for six months of the year nobody wants to wear more clothes than necessary.

(Poor Sister! She gets around every day in her heavy nun's habit. We know she must be roasting.)

What we can't understand and the teachers can't explain to us is the difference between black and white standards.

The weather is just as hot in Darwin, but there the white girls go to school in heavy uniforms.

You never see one of them dressed as we are, with bare breasts.

We are told it would be wrong for them to do so. Why, then, is it all right for us? Not that we mind; in fact, we prefer it this way.

Here you see about thirty of us from the Tiwi, Urangku, Tikalaru, Malau and Mandiupi tribes, studying the English language.

Parse this! Analyse that! What is a preposition? Who was Tennyson? How do you spell syzygy? Conjugate the verb To Learn.

Frankly, who cares?

We would like the answer to another question: How many white kids in Darwin are studying the Tiwi, Warramunga, Aranda, Anula and Goba-boingu tongues?

There are sixty separate aboriginal languages in the Northern Territory alone, and about two hundred dialects.

Don't you think the Darwin kids should start on a few of these before French and Latin?

The tribes who speak all these tongues are right here with us in our own country. Yet not more than a dozen white people have ever learnt to speak one of them.

France and Latin are thousands of miles away across the sea. We often wonder why people are taught to speak the language of people they will probably never see, but not taught the language of others who live with them.

You know, we wouldn't mind all this stuff half as much if we had parents who could help us with our homework.

The trouble is that if we ask our mothers the sum of six and seven they're likely to say 'Little bit big-feller mob.' If we ask them how to spell cat they say 'Meow'.

Please don't think we are complaining. On the contrary, we are conscious of a very great privilege. Our mothers and fathers had little or no schooling. But any aboriginal child who doesn't attend a school today must be living in a remote area where there are no schools. As late as nineteen hundred and fifty there were not many more than one hundred aboriginal students. Today there are about three thousand.

At several missions and settlements there have been one hundred per cent attendances. At Delissaville there was a percentage attendance of one hundred and twelve! That simply meant that a few over-age adults and under-age children went along too.

The first teachers faced almost insuperable problems. We would be getting along nicely in our first grades when our parents would decide to take us on annual Walkabout. That meant an absence of three months. The teachers had to accept the fact that they had no control over their pupils. If our parents decided that the turtle egg harvest was ready to be reaped at Shoal Bay, or the dugong season was in full swing at Millin-gimbi, they were unimpressed by the requirements of book learning. They picked up their spears and dillybags and began walking. We followed — with disastrous results when the examinations came around.

Now all that has changed. Most of us can read and write, parse and analyse.

Sister tells us that one day we will all grow up and have children of our own.

They will come home at night and say, 'Mum, how do you prove that the bisector of an angle of a triangle divides the opposite side in the ratio of the sides containing the angle?'

And we'll be able to say, 'I've forgotten, dear. It's a long time since I was at school. Anyway, Mummy's busy now.'

Hey, you there in the third seat of the centre row! Stop cheating!

Lookouts

LUNGA TRIBE

KIMBERLEYS, NORTH-WEST AUSTRALIA

UGH! UGH! PALEFACES!

There on the valley floor below. See their caravan moving slowly, the dust swirling high, betraying their position as accurately as if they had sent us a smoke signal.

Brothers, let us leave now and stalk them to an ambush in that defile yonder. We will gather at the farther end and wait there with our spears ready. Once the caravan has entered the gorge the car will be unable to turn. We will have them at our mercy.

They will have women and children, knives and tomahawks, food and tobacco and all the other loot so dear to our hearts.

And we will have our spears and our woomeras, boomerangs and nulla nullas. We must not let them escape.

Don't forget the exchange rate: One spear for a tin of tobacco; a spear, a woomera, a boomerang and a nulla nulla for a tomahawk; a boomerang for a knife; a nulla nulla for a tin of bully beef.

Watch they don't beat you out of a fair trade. Some of these New Australians are sharper than the Indians.

And keep your eyes on their kids, especially the boys. The thieving little brats would steal the Town Hall clock.

Thus have the British people reduced us to a nation of tradesmen.

There was a time when we took what we wanted. The white men and women who first violated our Australian countryside had to pay the price.

Many of them died in agony, struggling and kicking on the ends of our barbarous spears.

We raised human barriers west and north across the vast continent and disputed every inch of the invasion. Thomas Mitchell, Charles Sturt, John McDouall Stuart, Ludwig Leichhardt — these and a dozen other intrepid white explorers had to cope with us in addition to the dangers of the inhospitable terrain.

We gave them a torrid time.

But for us it was hell.

We were introduced to firearms — on the receiving end. Our men fell and died, struck down by unseen leaden arrows against which we had no chance.

Our valorous warriors soon learnt that it was better to be discreet.

Our lands were alienated and our waters denied us. Our women were molested. We were decimated by new diseases.

When the white man came to Australia the aboriginal people numbered 350,000.

Now we are 46,000.

Somewhere along the line more than 300,000 of our tribesmen have been lost.

In the same period of less than two hundred years the white population has grown from nought to ten million.

We died of tuberculosis, leprosy, venereal disease — and lead poisoning.

But chiefly we died spiritlessly, of broken hearts, because we didn't have the will to live.

Once upon a time the three of us might have used this vantage point to watch for game moving out to graze and thus begin our hunt for food.

We might have used it as a lookout in our brief war against the Europeans.

But today it is only one of the cliffs where we lie in wait for white men who carry the civilized opiums we covet.

Once we used our weapons to kill food. Now we use them chiefly as a means of barter.

It is unfortunately true that a growing number of aborigines living on the fringes of civilization don't know how to hunt. Their children will never know because they are learning to read and write instead.

That is not the case with the people who live in Arnhem Land or in other remote corners where the ability to track game, and then to hunt and kill it, is still part of the basic equipment of a man who must learn to survive by his wits and his spear-arm. In those places, much of the family diet still consists of kangaroo and goanna, or fish caught on three-pronged spears. The story is very different in towns like Darwin and Alice Springs, and even on some of the more accessible missions and settlements.

The emphasis there has changed from tracking and hunting to reading and writing. An aboriginal boy who spends ten years of his early life in school doesn't have much time to study the science of the bush . . . the art of survival which was handed down to us, without books, by our ancestors.

We invited one of them to come on a hunting walkabout with us. 'Thank you,' he said. 'Just wait till I get my weapon.' Presently he joined us — with a rifle and a box of bullets. We were shocked, and said so.

'Don't be so silly,' he said, with something less than respect. 'We'll see who gets the most kangaroos.'

That night we returned shamefaced and empty-handed. The hunt had been long and tiring . . . and we were hungry. The galling part of it was that we had to eat the kangaroo he shot, while he treated us with withering scorn.

'Only a fool would want to throw a spear when he can use a rifle,' he said.

Yet we wonder . . . we wonder who will best be able to live off the land if there should be another war and all the rifles and bullets are melted by nuclear fission.

203

The Watermen

MANDIUPI TRIBE

BATHURST ISLAND, N.T.

←――――――――――――――――――――――――――――――→

EXTEND THAT PROW UPWARDS, decorate it with a figurehead, give us each a lance and a helmet, and we could be Vikings sailing against England.

Mind you, we are inclined to believe that the Vikings were bits of cissies. Certainly they were fearless warriors. We always remember the man about to be beheaded who asked for a sword to be put in his hand and his bonds freed to prove a point they weren't sure about: whether a man could fight without his head. But when it came to making sailing ships for their 8th, 9th and 10th Century assaults against Britain, they seemed to be afraid of drowning.

Why, they had planks and keels in their ships, and crude forms of copper and iron, and everything was put together with nails!

No self-respecting aboriginal would put a nail near his canoe. If he did it would mean nothing less than that he had made a bad job of it in the first place — without nails.

Our dugout canoes are one solid piece of wood, laboriously chipped out of the trunk of a tree.

Building one is a long and tiresome job. It wouldn't be so bad if we always had proper adzes and axes, but sometimes we have to work with bits of old iron and discarded knives.

Normally the whole tribe takes a hand in the work. The finished craft belongs to all of us. And they are so heavy that it takes a tribe to launch one.

We have experts who, if given proper small axes, can make a canoe comfortably in one day.

The trouble with these dugouts is that they are terribly unstable. There is no keel, and the rounded log capsizes easily unless there is perfect co-ordination between the crewmen.

But that is all part of the fun. Fortunately they are unsinkable. When we get a ducking we simply turn it upright and clamber aboard again. We don't have to worry about drying out our clothes because, as you can see, we don't have many. And we've learnt by experience not to carry valuables in a dugout in rough weather.

A few centuries ago our only means of water transport was in bark canoes which were so frail that they broke apart in rough seas. That was very good for the sharks, but not so good for our ancestors.

A canoe like the one you see here can carry as many people as can squeeze into it. That might be fifteen or twenty. We've crossed van Diemen's Gulf from Bathurst Island to Darwin — about seventy miles — with a dozen men, women, piccaninnies and dogs aboard.

Some of our people do that regularly, just to go to the cinema. We are all addicts of horse operas. If there's a good wind blowing we can leave at dawn on Tuesday and be there for the pictures on Wednesday night. We go home again when the wind changes. That might be the following day or in a month's time. But it doesn't matter . . . time is one of the things we have plenty of.

We believe it was probably in craft such as these that the first aborigines came to Australia, perhaps from as far away as India and Ceylon. They may have been equipped with outriggers to give them stability; even so, it seems probable that many of them perished at sea.

Today we use the canoes simply as a means of transport, and as vessels to be used in our war-without-malice against barramundi, turtles, sting-rays and dugong.

The dugong are big sea mammals. Some weigh as much as half a ton. And we just happen to be partial to their flesh, whether grilled, baked, fried or stewed.

It's really delicious, perhaps resembling pork. As an old witchdoctor friend of ours once said: 'The nearest thing to human flesh I've ever tasted.'

S-s-s-h! There's a dugong now! Pardon us while we get a harpoon ready.

You'll notice that the harpoon is not attached to a rope. That's a lesson we learnt the hard way. Not long ago a few of us speared a big bull dugong. The harpoon was tied to a rope and attached to the bow of the canoe.

When he was struck, with the harpoon fast in his flesh, the dugong decided to take us on a Pacific cruise.

There we were, sitting up like Jackies, but unable to cut the line because we had no axe. We were doing eight knots in the direction of New Guinea when the dugong had reached full speed.

We may have been going yet — and the canoe probably is — except that we signalled our distress to tribesmen in another dugout and then all jumped overboard. They rescued us.

When relieved of the weight of six men, the dugong increased speed until he had that canoe aquaplaning on the water. Soon it was out of sight, and has never been seen again.

Some people don't believe that story, but it's true.

We can tell you this: These days we harpoon dugongs our own size. The really big fellows we leave alone. None of us is anxious to see New Guinea.

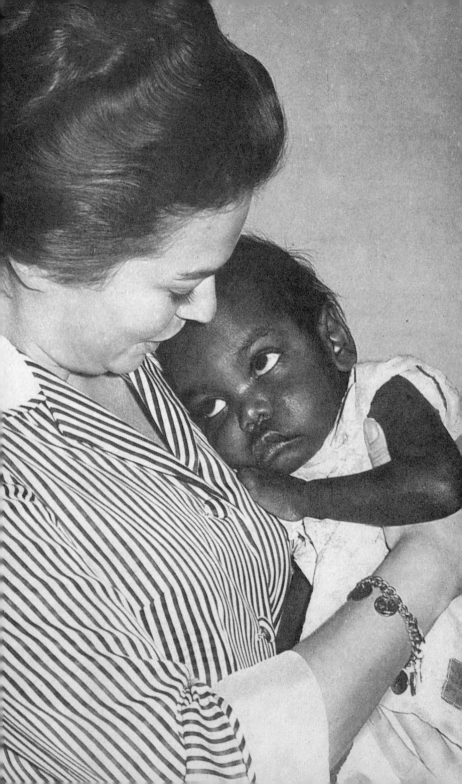

Baby Ben

ALAWA TRIBE

ROPER RIVER, N.T.

←——————————————————————————

ACTUALLY, I'M NOT nearly as coy or bashful as I seem.

It's a little disconcerting at first to be in the arms of Tricia Reschke, who was Miss Australia.

But you get used to it.

And when you do . . . oh boy! I'm in no hurry to leave.

I know a few white men who wouldn't mind swapping places with me.

As a matter of fact, one of them offered me an icecream if I could persuade Tricia to give him a cuddle.

I tried, because an icecream is pretty luscious, too.

But Tricia whispered to me that I should tell the guy to do his own asking.

Then she said to me: 'What's he like? Is he tall? Is he dark? Is he handsome?' She was interested, all right.

He is dark and handsome, too. And I know he did ask her for a cuddle later. Well . . . perhaps not a cuddle. It was at a grand ball in Darwin, with everyone done up in flash clothes, and this guy went to Tricia and he said, 'Will you dance with me, please?'

So she went straight into his arms, and they danced around together. Afterwards he had to leave her.

'Chaperones!' he growled.

But you should have seen the look on his face while they danced. Real dreamy. And I think she was doing a little dreaming, too.

'Nice man,' she said. 'He's got nice eyes.'

But, golly, you should see Tricia's eyes. They're grey, and almost as huge as mine. And she's built like a goddess.

Tricia came along to Darwin hospital especially to see me. Of course, I got a terrible ribbing later from the other kids about this cuddle, but I didn't mind. They're a jealous lot, if you ask me. And, frankly, it was well worthwhile. That bosom I'm resting my head on, for instance: I'm prepared to be quoted as saying that there's no false padding there. That's her.

One thing that surprised me was Tricia's language. As Miss Australia, I thought she would speak English. Yet there were many words I didn't understand. One was 'Diddums,' which she used constantly. They tell me it's baby-talk. Maybe she's practising for the time when she'll be trying it out on her own piccaninnies.

I hope she finds this right guy soon and gets married. I can only say that if their children are all girls and they're all as beautiful as their mother, Australia is going to be a great place for young men about twenty years from now.

Can you imagine her husband trying to cope with a family of teen-age daughters who have their mother's beauty?

I reckon he'd need a private telephone exchange in the house.

And he'd want to stay fighting fit for a few years.

We don't have beauty competitions in the tribes. For one thing — let's face it — we don't have much natural beauty, at least not by white standards.

Even the women who are attractive in their own way are badly outnumbered by the spindle-shanks, the skinny, and the pendulum-breasted.

Fortunately, physical beauty is a matter of indifference to our men. They adhere strictly to the view that as long as a woman can bear burdens and bear children she is adequate. Her physical appearance is of little importance. But among the young women, especially around Darwin, there is a growing awareness that they can look quite attractive if they groom themselves properly — a regular hair wash, a neatly pressed frock preferably of one strong colour, and bare feet.

Yes, bare feet! Our women just don't seem to be able to wear shoes. Fashionable shoes make them ridiculous. I suppose it's because they have always been barefooted. They walk erectly, and beautifully, but the moment they put shoes on it seems that they are cripples. In any case, on aboriginal feet they look wrong. What's more, a woman wearing shoes loses two of her hands. She can no longer pick up stones or scraps of food with her toes.

Perhaps it is just as well that our lives are not complicated by beauty and all it leads to. We have enough to fight about without that.

The judges in any Miss Warramunga Quest would need to come well armed.

They say there can be only one winner of any competition. That may be true, but the number of losers can often be more than expected, and include all the judges. You'd know what I meant if you saw the nulla-nullas carried by the relatives at our tournaments.

Minyina

WAILBRI TRIBE

YUENDUMU, N.T.

Amidst the purple heath a tribesman lies,
  A weary elder of a vanished clan.
The warm breeze through the brown acacia sighs
  A chant of springtime for the lone old man.

But spring has gone for him, and now he dreams
  Of campfires flickering with the evening breeze,
Of children shouting by the inland streams,
  Of hunting lizards on their dusty knees.

He saw the white-men riding down a track
  Into his tribal lands. Then came the ring
Of axe on tree. He heard the stock whips crack
  And knew that he no longer was the king.

As youth and age went drifting down the ways,
  And tribal life was shattered, he remained
Amidst the ritual of departed days,
  Taught to the young, and by the old explained.

He watched the tribal elders pass away,
  And with them went the ancient Dreamtime lore
That held the tribes in bond . . . in wide decay
  Only the land remained. . . . And never-more

213

Shall totem-heroes stride with roaring cries
    Along the creeks, the valleys and the hills,
No more shall Rain-men battle in the skies,
    Or Frog-men croak for rain as magic kills

The unbeliever who, with pride and scorn,
    Laughed at the tribal lore, and mocked its powers.
Now ritual has gone, and here forlorn
    An old man sleeps amidst the wild bush flowers.

Blindness, scurvy, yaws and malnutrition have always been high on the list of misfortunes that Central Australian aborigines have to bear.

I am Minyina, a seventy-year-old member of the Wailbri tribe. It is many years since I have seen the sun, for I am totally blind. The dreaded trachoma, a virulent sandy blight which scars the eyes with granular excrescences, has eaten away the irises and pupils.

That was in the days before we had regular medical aid in this part of the world. I suffered pain day and night for longer than I care to remember while the insidious disease slowly pulled a blind over the sun forever.

Dozens of my tribal friends suffered with me. You don't have to look far in the desert to find a man who is blind. But you will also notice that most of them are old men. The younger ones are treated with the magic white-feller medicine before the damage has gone too far.

The white man has brought us many such blessings, especially in the field of medicine. In the big drought which lasted from 1926 until 1930, hundreds of my people died from scurvy. We were then alone in the desert, cut off from fresh fruit and vegetables. The gums of the afflicted bled so freely that they were prostrated and died. Simple malnutrition killed many others.

Now the white man prevents these things from happening. We have had no scurvy for twenty years, and trachoma is less troublesome.

Even so, I sometimes wonder how much this solicitude for our welfare is dictated by a guilty conscience. I am grateful for what is being done for my people. And yet I cannot forget the diabolical cruelties which were inflicted on me and the men of my generation by the early settlers.

It is not so long ago that a white man trussed me up like a fowl with a leather surcingle and beat me with sticks and greenhide thongs. Later he tied me to a tree with a bullants' nest at its base and a greenants' nest in its leaves.

Why? Because I had camped on the bank of a waterhole which he said we must not use. 'The cattle need it,' he said.

This had always been one of our watering places. Then the government gave the land to the pastoralists and their cattle. We were to be chased off.

It was during this period that tens of thousands of our tribesmen died. By the time the sense of guilt began to prick it was almost too late.

All of the tribes had been decimated and scattered.

We became human blowflies, living on the scrapheaps and woodheaps of the new civilization.

The rehabilitation programme now being undertaken is costing millions of pounds. Entire tribes have had to be housed and settled in new areas. Underground water has had to be found and brought to the surface with pumps, then laid to our camps with pipes and pumps.

This is our compensation: that we can now get water at any time just by turning a tap.

We get medical aid for ourselves and our children.

The government will send the Flying Doctor plane hundreds of miles to evacuate the lowliest piccaninny whose illness cannot be cured or diagnosed by the resident Sister.

Conscience is a wonderful thing — once it begins to work.

Hamilton Downs Johnnie

ARANDA TRIBE

ALICE SPRINGS, N.T.

←——————————————————————

MY ENTIRE LIFE HAS been spent in the service of white men. I've been with them through two generations.

Things were tough in the early days of settlement in this district, but I must say that for the past twenty-five years I have been well looked after.

There is a lot of criticism in this book about our maltreatment by squatters.

I have read Topsy's shameful story about the way her people were forced into cannibalism, and Minyina's yarn of cruelty.

I have read the piteous tale of exploitation told by Jackson. He wasn't the only one among us who traded gold for flour and was blinded by dust and trachoma.

Many more of my people have been cruelly misused.

And yet it is not true to say that that was our common lot, even in the bad old days.

Today it would be quite untrue.

You may think you see in my face a similarity to Bertrand Russell's. He is always being sorry for the future of the human race, just as I am sorry for its past. Perhaps our grief, one prospective and the other retrospective, has caused our souls to be reflected in our faces.

But I am not an unhappy man. My life has been much easier than it otherwise would simply because the white men came here and selected our lands for cattle. Of course, many of the theoreticians on the aborigines, few of whom have ever been here, will disagree with that.

Consider the alternatives:

A century ago we lived and died with bellies that were more often empty than full. In the summer and especially in the long droughts we seldom had enough to drink. Our children were emaciated and ravished by scurvy. We were human animals, primitive in the extreme, eating rats and mice, lizards and snakes, and fighting clannish wars over our hunting territories. The country was too poor to sustain us properly.

It is not far from where I live at Hamilton Downs, in the glorious shadows of the MacDonnell Ranges, to the deserts west of Haast Bluff and Yuendumu.

My bosses at Hamilton Downs, Damian Miller and Pat Davis and Bill Prior, raise fat cattle. Just to think of those rumps and fillets makes my spear-arm itchy — really a token of man's instinct to hunt and kill his own food, because these white men see to it that there is never any shortage of beef in my tucker bags.

The long plains stretching up to the foothills of the MacDonnells are covered in Mitchell grass and succulent herbage. In the droughts — and they come regularly — there is an abundance of what is called 'top feed.' That, chiefly, consists of the leaves of mulga trees and suplejack; these are so nutritious that cattle live on them for years, and even grow fat in country where there is not a blade of grass to be seen. I have often been out on mulga-cutting expeditions, bringing down branches in the bad times when the cattle have grazed the trees until the leaves are out of reach. But, you know, I have a feeling that cattle would never die on Hamilton Downs; when all else failed they could live on scenery — the magnificent blues, reds and purples that Albert Namatjira perpetuated!

Further west, of course, it is a different story. Out past Haast Bluff and Yuendumu you run into what might be described as Proper Black-feller Country; arid wastes of spinifex and sand where, nevertheless, the Wailbri and Pintubi tribes lived and hunted and somehow multiplied. They had more meal-times than meals. Obesity was never a problem among them. The diet of rats and mice, lizards and snakes, was almost unchanging.

218

But when the white man came he brought cattle, flour, baking soda, tea and tinned food. There was not much of the tinned food for us at first, although there is plenty today — but we were never short of bread and beef, even if we had to steal it.

In a land where water was scarce the white men bored down into the earth and soon had it flowing miraculously into tanks and troughs from underground rivers. Since then only the silliest among us have ever died of thirst.

I would like to put it on record that my employers have always been kind to me. I was an asset to them, naturally. I was a head-stockman. I knew all there was to know about working cattle. I was in charge of a group of my tribesmen. For many years I supervised the mustering, the branding, the castrating, the horse-breaking and all the other realities of stockwork.

I liked it. I was given a home on the property. My wife and family were cared for. I had all I needed of the only security we understood — plenty of food, water and shelter.

When I was too old to work my employers gave me a place to live and have continued to feed me. They will do so until I die. They even promoted me to 'King' Johnnie.

Most of this talk about maltreatment, especially as it refers to past generations, is regrettably true.

But we should keep the record straight. That kind of thing is not happening today and in my case it never happened. I have had a good life, thanks to the white man. And I'm not the only one, either.

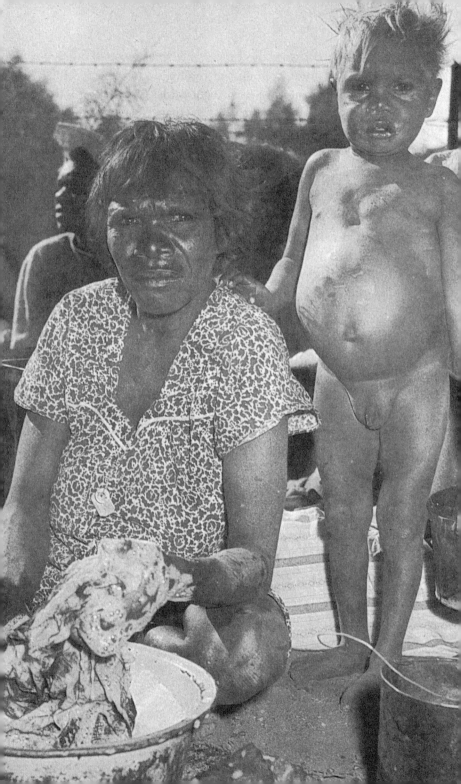

Biddy

WAILBRI TRIBE

YUENDUMU, N.T.

←———————————————————————————————

CIVILIZATION IS ALL VERY well for women who have automatic washing machines. But I'm the washing machine in this family, and I can tell you that I'm sick and tired of it.

Every Monday morning I yearn for those uncivilized days when the entire Wailbri tribe — men, women and piccaninnies — were naked.

There were then no clothes to wash, no ironing, no mending, no sewing.

Now look at me! Caught in a never-ending labour that should be quite unnecessary.

Do you know why we are wearing clothes after doing without them for generations?

Because the white man has come. He thinks the human body is offensive and should at all times remain covered. We must hide it from him.

He cannot bring himself to regard nakedness as natural. In fact he has laws to prevent it. Anyone convicted of exposing a body to view can be sent to gaol. (Although I'm not so sure that the evil isn't often in the eye of the beholder. I've seen men watching furtively as a woman uncovers her breast to feed a child, or removes a dress to wash it.)

For some inexplicable reason it is not considered offensive for small children to be naked. Hence Michael, my son, is in no danger of prosecution.

But my older children are all fully covered. My pile of washing has become mountainous.

However, I shouldn't be grumbling like this. I suppose it is something that we are given clothes at all. There is no doubt that the government has at last taken note of our existence and is doing everything possible to make sure we don't vanish from the face of the earth, as once seemed likely.

If for no other reason, I am grateful for the change in my children's physique. When my eldest two were born we were still primitive nomads hunting in the desert. Every day I had to watch them slowly starving. Their legs were like sticks, their bellies hollow, their mouths often bleeding with scurvy.

But look at Michael's belly. He eats so much good food that it's running out his ears. When he walks he waddles, throwing his shoulders back as a counter-balance to the weight he is carrying out front.

My washing-day blues are always dispelled when I think of these things and realize that if I have another dozen children none of them will ever be hungry. Washing clothes also means that we have plenty of water. Only a decade ago, drinking from our desert seeps, this would have been wanton waste.

Now we fill the buckets from taps that never run dry.

That barbed wire in the rear?

Oh no, that's not to keep us in.

That is to keep the white men out.

It is necessary for a white man to have a permit to visit any Government settlement or mission station in the Northern Territory.

Once upon a time they chased us away from their waters. Now we have a few waters inside reservations, and it is our turn to do the chasing.

Not that the reserves include much good cattle country. Ah, no! That was all taken long ago, before permits became necessary. Most of the land left to us is barren; either desert country in the great south-west reserve, or the forbidding escarpments of Arnhem Land.

Even so, there have been complaints recently about us having this land. They've been saying in the Legislative Council and elsewhere that too much of Australia is wasted on the blackfellers. Well, we have about ninety-five thousand square miles in the Territory. More than forty thousand square miles of that is in the south-west reserve, and thirty thousand in Arnhem Land.

Mind you, if anything valuable is found on an aboriginal reserve it seems possible for us to be pushed aside without consultation. There was the recent example of a bauxite discovery at Gove in north-eastern Arnhem Land. Apparently this mineral is valuable for making aluminium, and some big company men went along to see it. The result was that the part containing the bauxite was turned over as a mineral lease and we are to be paid a royalty. But here's the point: Nobody asked US whether WE wanted the land transferred.

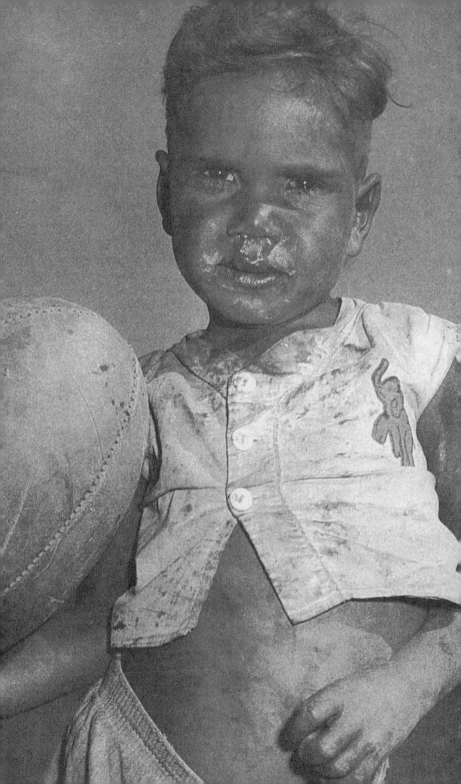

Danny

WAILBRI TRIBE

YUENDUMU, N.T.

←———————————————————————————————

GEE, MISTER, DID YOU see me roll that feller? I ran alongside and gave him the old shoulder when he was off balance. I'll bet he somersaulted eight times before he stopped rolling. Took yards of skin off his elbows and knees. Then he came at me again trying to tackle me around the ankles. I turned and put my head down and butted him in the belly. He hasn't come back for more. Last I saw of him he was crying like a baby and running for his Mumma. The great big sook!

When those Pintubi kids come here to play football with the Wailbris they want to remember that we're made of really tough stuff. This ball is bigger than my chest but that doesn't mean I can't kick it with my bare feet like my father and my big brothers. And it doesn't mean I can't kick those Pintubi kids in the shins, either.

You might think it wouldn't hurt to be kicked in the shins by a bare-footed boy. If so, I can only say that you've never been kicked by a Wailbri. Our feet are like iron. They must be to stand up to the hard wear and tear: racing over bindy-eyes and the porcupine-spinifex bush educates the skin to toughness very quickly.

Let me introduce myself: I'm Danny, captain of the Wailbri Five-and-Under team. If somebody said to me, 'Danny, would you rather go to Alice Springs or stay here at Yuendumu to play football?' I would unhesitatingly choose the game of footy.

There was a time when we played other games: making false tracks of animals to fool other kids and sometimes our fathers; climbing the mulga trees for bird nests; pulling live snakes apart, and gentle diversions of that nature.

Then one day a man brought a football out here and taught us how to play. We've been addicts ever since.

We play Australian Rules, which seems to us to be a happy medium between Soccer, which is a kind of tiggy-touchwood, and Rugby, which is legalized brawling.

Mind you, the Soccer and Rugby fans are just as scornful of Aussie Rules. They call it aerial ping-pong.

But, oh boy, it's a great game. There are so many things you can do when the umpire has his back turned, like giving a feller an elbow in the solar plexus or putting your knees in his kidneys when you're flying for a high mark.

You apologize profusely, of course, which makes it look like an accident, but the effect is the same: he loses a lot of interest in the game and is thereafter inclined to watch you rather than the ball. A white kid who was here taught me these tricks (I hope you didn't think any aboriginal would invent them?)

We've got some great players. Ted Cooper, whose photo is in this book, once had a run with Fitzroy in the Melbourne League. He couldn't stand the cold. David Kantilla is a ruckman for South Adelaide in the Adelaide League.

Our players shine best in their own environment. You should see some of the Bathurst Islanders who form the greater part of the St. Mary's team in the N.T. League at Darwin. You've never seen anything like their high-flying! And nippy! Like greased lightning.

'Up there, Stanislaus!' they yell. They have to say that; in the heat of the moment they could not be expected to say, 'Up there, Tampialapat-jimi!' which is his proper name.

How could the barrackers keep up with the game if they had to say, 'Go through there, Pilimapitjimiri!' He's a great player, too, but his footy name is Sylvester.

Can you imagine a barracker giving this kind of advice to Urban, another St. Mary's player: 'Get a bag, Tipaklariua, you drongo!'?

Or 'Go back to South Adelaide, Amparralamtua!'? (David Kantilla.)

In fact, if the coach had to call the tribal names of the St. Mary's team they'd reach the ground at half time.

In Central Australia we play footy in the winter. But those stupid northerners play in the tropical heat of the wet season: the average is about 95 degrees, with 70% to 80% humidity. 'The ground is soft. It's better for the gravel rash,' they say.

You reckon my nose is running. No, no, that's blood. Can't you see it all over my shirt? I had a bit of an argument with the ball. One of my mates stab-kicked it to me just as the sun got in my eyes and the ball got in my nose and mouth. It made me mad. I jumped up, ran in the wrong direction, put out my hands to steady myself, and found the ball sticking to them. The cheering was deafening as I ran in and kicked a goal. You should have heard the noise! It was quite a while before I found out I had kicked through the wrong goals.

Ah, well. Come out and watch us play sometimes. Admission is free, although it will cost you about ten pounds for petrol to drive from Alice Springs. We use a couple of mulga trees for goal posts. The ground is pitted with anthills and stumps, but we dodge around them. The spinifex punctures the ball occasionally.

But you'll have fun, like we do.

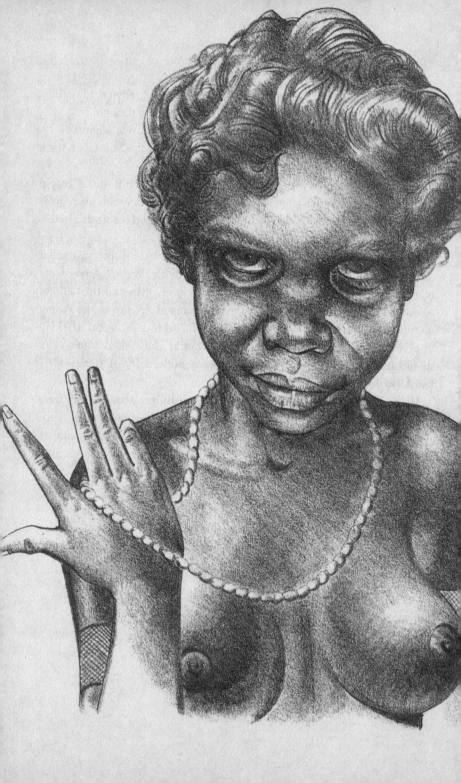

Buckjumper Jinnie

BRINKEN TRIBE

NEAR DARWIN, N.T.

⟵――――――――――――――――――――――――――

I like to love the Asian girl, the lass from Manila makes eyes,
The lubra grins in her nakedness, the half-caste laughs and lies,
The Javanese are not bad sorts, the Jap and the Chinese maid,
Zulu and Kaffir and Hottentot, they're all of an A1 grade.

BUT

The bushman's gin is a very fine thing,
   A very fine thing to have,
Twinkling eyes and gleaming teeth, eyes to shock an Irish priest,
   Ways that are always knave,
Rollicking, rolling, rollicking, rolling, real Australian maid.

The Australian nigger's a lazy beggar, he sits in the shade all day,
Won't hunt tucker. His wife is clever. She'll give your tucker away.
He sits in the shade his lubra made, far better than the white
   feller man,
You may think you're clever, but by hell you'll never get the
   better of her benjiman.

AND

The bushman's gin is a very fine thing,
   A very fine thing to have.

Come on up and see me sometime.
  We can lie here in the sand for awhile and you can whisper to me
about love — that word another white man taught me.

229

He said, 'Jinnie, your skin is like bronze. Your hair is like black silk. Your breasts are like ripe papaws. Your eyes are brooding pools of indigo which melt the marrow in my bones.'

He was really a funny guy, but I liked him and his talk.

And did he like me? Oh, brother!

'Buckjumper Jinnie,' he called me. I never knew why, but sometimes I heard him talking about me to other stockmen. That was the name he always used.

You know, every woman likes to be made a fuss of, whatever her colour.

That's one of the reasons I've always been fond of white men. That — and the money, of course.

I've got a dilly bag full of dresses back at the camp. Some of them are very pretty. All given to me by my admirers. Not that I have much use for them out here in the bush. I go around naked like this most of the time. The sun is warm and the wind is soft and it's nice to feel both playing over my body.

Nevertheless, a girl wants something decent to wear in Darwin. The police wouldn't be amused if I walked up and down the main street like this. Nor would some of the Mrs. Grundys who live in the flash suburbs.

I could tell you a thing or two about those places. I used to work there, in a big home.

The job didn't suit me, so I walked out. Every time the Missus went away and left me at home with The Boss he wanted to play about.

Lots of other black girls around town had the same trouble.

Not that I'm a prude, or anything, but I always say there is a time and place for everything. What do you always say?

Some of the white bosses I knew were about as subtle in their approach to love as the old cartoon-blackfellers who knocked their women on the head with nulla-nullas and dragged them off to the nearest cave.

They seemed to think that a black housegirl was a chattel who should submit without question when the Bigfeller Boss beckoned towards the bedroom.

What annoyed me most was that they were so terribly ashamed of themselves afterwards, as though they had committed a criminal act.

They hated us while they loved us. They hated their own inability to resist what they insultingly called Black Velvet.

It's much better out here in the bush.

The stockmen, the bagmen, the prospectors and the white hunters have no such inhibitions.

They want us, they know how to get us, and they're not appalled by it.

And out here I don't have to worry about my nudity.

I wear clothes or go naked, depending only on the weather.

'Indecent exposure,' the white men call it.

Exposure of the body? Or exposure of the mind?

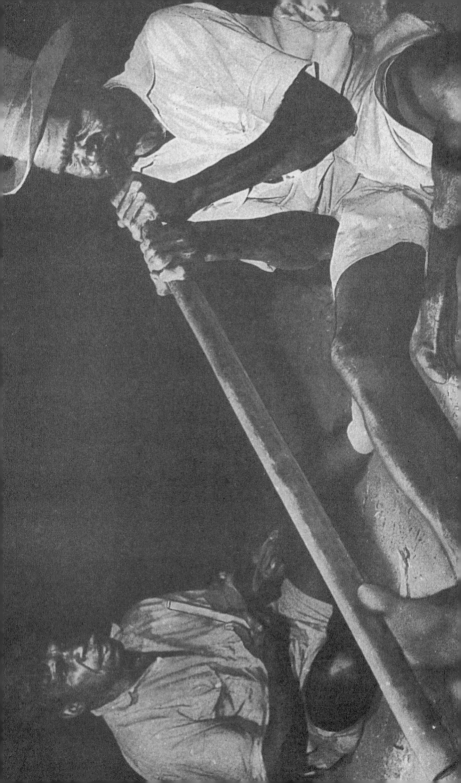

The Musician

WARGITE TRIBE

DARWIN, N.T.

←————————————————————————————

THE DIDGEREDOO, ONE OF the few aboriginal musical instruments, is a true woodwind.

There is nothing more to it than wood and wind and yet I've never known a white man who could play one.

In fact, not all aborigines can play the didgeredoo, and that has led to some profound remorse among us. It is our instrument and we should all be able to play it. There is no great technique involved once the player has solved the problem of being able to produce continuous sound — or sound of any kind. To some, this comes easily. To others it appears to be an impossibility and that causes them great frustration, especially as the instrument is so widely used in our corroborees, whether they are symbolic rituals or interpretative dances.

I have known aboriginal men to practise with the didgeredoo from dawn to dark, week after week for many months, and never once make a sound that wasn't made with the human voice. They are irritated by the scorn and laughter of their friends, and infuriated when they see a ten-year-old boy put an enormous pipe to his mouth and make glorious musical notes.

We have known men to hide in the bush, practising for days in secret, but with the same result. When they were discovered in these secret attempts the laughter of the tribesmen was louder, and the inept musician was propelled into wilder fury. To watch one of them in action, without him knowing he is being watched, is an hilarious spectacle. He huffs and

233

puffs, pouts and poses, trying various methods with his mouth and tongue, almost bursting himself with effort — yet getting nothing but wind from the didgeredoo.

It's all in the way you hold your mouth.

Most woodwinds have refinements like reeds and keys which are used with the tongue and fingers to produce musical notes. The didgeredoo is simply a hollowed log about five feet long and three inches in diameter.

There are only two holes — one to fit the mouth over and the other for the noise to come out.

It can be made to produce a plaintive, haunting melody not unlike the bass note of a pipe organ. And, like a Congo drum, the sound it makes carries much further than the average musical instrument.

A didgeredoo played at Delissaville settlement can often be heard in Darwin, about six miles away.

It is, of course, the musical centre-piece of most of the corroborees danced by the northern tribes in The Territory and the East Kimberleys.

The 'puller', as he is called, plays endlessly through the night as The Songman with his beating sticks taps out his rhythm and the dancers' feet pound the earth into powdered dust.

As you can see, the big toe is important. Without it I would feel as deprived as a fiddler without his bow. It also acts as a kind of music stand.

There is, however, one drawback to all this: I am prevented by my position from beating time with my feet. Any of the great musicians will tell you how serious a handicap that can be.

It would never do for Satchmo Armstrong or Fats Waller. Most of the famous jazz artists, in fact, would be struck dumb if they had to keep their feet quiet.

We had some fun one time at Delissaville with an American dancer named Ted Shawn who had come to study our dances so that he could interpret them on the stages of the world.

On the first night Ted walked down the hill from the settlement homestead to the corroboree ground. The deep bass of the didgeredoo was already filling the air with its rhythmic beat and the Songman was chanting an overture while the dancers prepared to go into their act.

As Ted approached we could see that he was absorbed by the primitive melody. We knew that he was a famous man, so we decided to give him an unusual welcome.

When he was a few yards from the didgeredoo Shawn stopped in his tracks and said, 'Listen! What's that thing saying?' He was told that it was a didgeredoo playing for the corroboree about to begin.

'I know that — but what is it saying?' he demanded.

His face had drained white. His flesh was covered with goose pimples. His eyes were staring ahead as though he didn't see. He was enraptured.

'Listen!' he demanded again. 'What's it saying?' And then we told him. The two beats to a bar plainly resolved themselves into 'Ted Shawn! Ted Shawn!'

'My God!' Shawn said. 'I'm back with my ancestors. This is terrific.'

The simple explanation was that the didgeredoo, in the hands of an expert, can be made to articulate one-syllable words. This was our tribute to the great white dancer — but Shawn had gone primitive. He believed in that moment that his spirit was linked somewhere in the past with the spirit of the aborigines who were now calling to him through their music.

Later he danced for us — to the drone of the didgeredoo.

Sugarbag Jack

WAILBRI TRIBE

YUENDUMU, N.T.

←————————————————————————————————

I SAW AN ASTONISHING thing the other day. A white man came out here to Yuendumu settlement with a collection of boomerangs he had made on a lathe.

And do you know that when he threw one it returned to his feet.

I've never seen anything so accurate in my life.

A lot of people think that every boomerang thrown by an aboriginal hunter returns to him.

I don't know where they got that idea but no boomerang I've ever thrown has returned to me — and I've been hunting with them all my life.

When I throw one I have to walk after it. I wish I could discover the white man's secret.

The boomerang, essentially, is nothing more than a throwing stick which has been curved so that it will travel in a straight line. When you've been tracking a kangaroo in the hot sun all day and then have to kill it with a stick you don't want the weapon to deviate from its true course.

If that happened it might be a long time between meals.

The Pintubi tribesmen out west from here are boomerang throwing experts. They can hit a small target at thirty yards with every shot.

You may be interested to know that the aborigines still have what is probably the oldest secret weapon in the world. Years ago the Djingali, the Waddaman and the Mudbra tribesmen fought with a fearsome hooked boomerang which was as superior to the conventional weapon as the hydrogen bomb is to T.N.T.

Originally the ordinary boomerang, like the one I'm about to throw, was a lethal weapon against our enemies. But they were also using it against us, so we had to invent a defence.

This was the wooden shield held in front of the body to deflect the boomerangs. It played the part of a portable tree behind which we could take cover.

Later we had the nulla-nulla, a heavy straight stick we used both as a weapon of offence and defence. It could be thrown, or used as a narrow shield.

But then some primitive genius invented the warradulla, a most diabolical weapon. This was a boomerang with a hook on the end, connected to the main body of the weapon by a wooden isthmus.

The theory of the warradulla was that the very act of stopping its flight with a shield or nulla-nulla caused the hooked end to fly off at tremendous speed, decapitating or seriously injuring its victim.

You want to watch out for the man who has one of them – he's dangerous.

My name, incidentally, is Sugarbag Jack of the Wailbri tribe. I've lived all my life in the desert and I will be here until I die.

Do you want to buy a good boomerang, Mister? Only ten bob. Or I can do you three for a quid. Brand new, all my own work, made from mulga wood. Genuine killing variety. They'd charge you a couple of quid each for them in Woolworths.

What d'ya say?

I suppose most people would say the boomerang has few advantages over a rifle when it comes to hunting kangaroos. Nevertheless, there is a reason – and it's an impressive one: a kangaroo can't turn a boomerang against the thrower, whereas it can fire a rifle.

You don't believe it? Then listen to the story of Arthur Crosbie, a half-caste stockman at Tipperary station, who has a six-inch bullet wound in the back of his right upper-arm.

'I was in Tipperary stockcamp,' Crosbie says. 'Kangaroos were coming into water. We were short of beef. I thought there'd be nothing wrong

238

with fresh 'roo steak and maybe a pot of 'roo-tail soup. So I went down with the rifle and shot one. It flew into the air, then sprawled on the ground. I ran over to the spring to bring him back, and reloaded the rifle on the way, thinking I might get another.

'When I got there the 'roo was still alive so I took aim to finish it off. But then I remembered we had only half a dozen bullets left. They were precious. A big waddy was lying near the kangaroo's head and I decided to kill it with that rather than waste a bullet.

'I jammed the butt of the rifle on its throat, holding its head so it couldn't move, then reached down to pick up the stick. While I was doing that the kangaroo got a paw around the trigger and pulled. I jumped about ten feet . . . the bullet went right through my arm. You know, just six inches to the right and he'd have got me through the chest. Nobody would have believed the story and my wife, who was with me, may have been on a murder charge.

'I've shot hundreds of kangaroos for tucker but this was the first one ever shot me,' Crosbie said.

Now do you see that a boomerang is safer?

Ngarla Kunoth

PART-ABORIGINAL

ALICE SPRINGS, N.T.

◀─────────────────────────────────────

WAS IT JUST A dream, or did it happen? Was my name in lights in front of the cinemas? Did I hear people whispering, 'There goes the star' Or was that a dream, too?

'No, Ngarla, it happened,' I assured her.

Well, it certainly all seems like a dream now, but a very beautiful dream. I remember that day long ago when Charles and Elsa Chauvel came to see me at St. Mary's Hostel in Alice Springs. I was cleaning out the fireplace. I was only fourteen and still going to school, but I had always been a big girl.

'Magnificent bosom,' I heard one of the photographers say.

'Classic profile,' another said.

They turned me around, examined my eyes and teeth and hair, made me smile, laugh, and speak until I felt like an exhibit in a show ring.

I knew they were looking for a film star, but they went away without telling me whether or not I had been chosen.

For days afterwards I couldn't concentrate on my lessons. My teacher was cross but couldn't make out what was wrong with me.

I was happy, wistfully dreaming that one day I would be famous . . . well, like Garbo.

Then they came back and offered me the part. I was to play the name role in 'Jedda', the first Australian film in colour.

I was terribly excited. I couldn't sleep. I couldn't work. Nothing

241

mattered except that I was to leave school and go away to be trained as a film star.

Little me! Rosie Kunoth. Ah, yes, *Rosie*. That would never do, of course. Whoever heard of a star with a name like that?

Charles and Elsa Chauvel set out to change me completely. They began with my name, which became Ngarla. The 'g' is silent. I was dressed in new clothes. My hair style was changed and so was my entire personality.

But do you know what happened to all those lovely clothes? They were put away. In the film, as you can see on the opposite page, I was dressed in rags! Here was I, thinking that I would be dressed like Cleopatra in exotic robes. Instead, I had to look like any other aboriginal girl, in a torn blouse and a tattered skirt. Oh, I could have screamed!

I ceased to be a shy coloured girl with a black mother and a halfcaste father. (That's my Aranda mother in the picture with me.)

I went before the cameras with other actors and actresses, but it was me, Ngarla, who was the star.

My leading man was Robert Tudawali, an aboriginal from Darwin. In the film he abducted me and took me away to the lonely places . . . until he went mad.

It was all great fun. I was taken on a grand tour around the big cities. I had never seen a town bigger than Alice Springs. I had to hold on to Elsa Chauvel to avoid being lost.

She took me into magic shops where I whizzed up and down on moving staircases. Wonderful places laden with dresses and hats and shoes and scrumptious things to eat.

'Cut out the apple pie and icecream,' Elsa ordered when she saw my waistline disappearing. My dresses wouldn't fit.

Did you see the picture?

'Yes, Ngarla, I saw the picture,' I said. 'You were great.'

Thanks, thanks. I'm glad you liked it. A pity it had to end like this. It was a moment . . . a brief moment. I've kept one or two things. Like Garbo, I have my memories.

'What are you doing now, Ngarla?' I asked.

Why, haven't you heard?

I'm a nun.

Yes, I'm never likely to be in films again. I'm devoting my life to the service of other people.

I've heard that Robert Tudawali has fallen on bad times. Give him my best wishes. He was a great actor . . . what they call 'a natural.' The director had to tell him once only, and he was perfect; perhaps too perfect for it seems to have gone to his head.

"As I appeared in the film . . . I could have screamed."

Blacktrackers

PITJENTJARRA TRIBE

CENTRAL AUSTRALIA

←————————————————————————————————

Where were you last night, Mister?

Now, now, there's no need to tell such outrageous lies.

How do we know you're lying? Listen, Mister, we could tell you a few things you don't even know about yourself.

Such as? Well, such as the fact that the heel of your right shoe is worn down more than the heel of your left shoe. Such as the fact that you're pigeon-toed only in the right foot. Did you know that you've scuffed the metal plate off the left heel but not off the right?

By the way, Mister, how's Virginia?

Virginia?

Yes, Virginia, the halfcaste girl. You visited her last night — after midnight.

We're sure, yes. We're sure of the time, too. The rain stopped at midnight. If you had arrived earlier your tracks would've been washed out.

Is that where you hid the loot, Mister? Okay, okay, no need to get nasty. We'll find it sooner or later and lead the white policemen to it.

It's no good denying that you took the stuff. Mister. We've got you cold. If you want some advice, we'd suggest you always smoke tailor-made cigarettes in future. Those roll-your-owns are a give-away.

Look at the one you're smoking now. See how you've curled the end of the paper to stop the tobacco spilling into your mouth? Now look at this one. It's exactly the same. Picked it up in the warehouse beside a pigeon-toed right footmark.

You're dealing with two of the best men in the force, Mister. You'd be surprised at what we know about who visits whom in this town.

Puddin' Lee was over at the railway cottages last night looking for Buckjumper Jinnie. We don't care how many of the black girls he sneaks after at night, but if he wants to keep it quiet he should throw away those crepe soles. He might as well send us a telegram about where he's going.

Snowy Baker was down the beach with Airy Fairy Mary. Both took their shoes off before they got out of the car, but if he wants his amours to remain anonymous he should change that front driving-side tyre. Good idea to match it up with the others, then the tracks won't look like a main road back to his garage.

Yeah, we've been at this game quite a while. You didn't know about it, but it was us who put the cops on to you after that job at the jewellery store last year.

Of course, this comes naturally to us. Our people have been professional trackers for generations. If we hadn't been able to identify and follow tracks the entire tribe would have starved long ago.

If you marched every blackfeller in Alice Springs past us, separately, we'd be able to identify them all after one look at their barefooted tracks. We're not boasting, Mister; that's just the plain truth.

We had one tracker named Black Syd who was uncanny at following a man's tracks through the bush *before he made them*.

You think that is impossible? So did we until Black Syd demonstrated that it was really quite easy.

Black Syd was a student of human behaviour. If you know what a man is likely to do in a given situation your battle is half won. Black Syd saved himself much time and bother by being at a wanted man's destination *when he arrived*.

Perhaps he was an aboriginal murderer who meticulously obliterated his tracks as he travelled. That didn't help much when Black Syd was on the job, especially if the murderer was known to him. He would go out by aeroplane or truck to the man's tribal country, then double back for a few miles and lie hidden at the edge of a billabong where he knew the man walking back home must stop for a drink. Great was the surprise when Black Syd approached with a gun and a pair of handcuffs.

On one occasion the police asked Black Syd to trace a vehicle used in a burglary. No tyre tracks were visible near the scene but he found the imprint of a rubber shoe with distinctive marks. For many weeks after that he studied taxis, watching the drivers getting in and out, until he found one with shoes which matched the tracks. He took the number and gave it to the police. The files showed the man had a criminal record. And when they visited his house they found the stolen goods.

'I bin do 'im easy,' Black Syd said.

Old Bul-Bul, who was the best tracker we ever had, once followed Nemarluk for nine months before he caught him. Nemarluk and his mates murdered five Japanese, but Bul-Bul got him in the end.

Then when Nemarluk escaped from gaol Bul-Bul chased him again — this time for twelve months. You've got to remember that Nemarluk himself was a hawk-eyed tracker and was often tracking Bul-Bul. But the old master outwitted him and got the manacles on him one night while he slept.

Well now, Mister, would you like to make a statement? Remember that anything you say will be written down and used in evidence against you.

Spear Fight

PINTUBI TRIBE

CENTRAL AUSTRALIA

←————————————————————————————————

GOT HIM! GARN, LIE down, lie down! You're dead Namatjira! You're dead Pareroultja! You're dead Inkamala! I got you fair in the guts!

Ah, the big bunch of cheats, they won't lie down when we get 'em. I speared Herbie Namatjira in the belly, didn't I, Mister? But look at him: he's still running around throwing spears back at me.

Namatjira, you play the game by the rules or else go home. We don't want to play with you, Namatjira. You're just as bad as some of those stupid white kids when they play Cops and Robbers. They won't lie down when they're shot, either.

Garn! Pooh to you, too. Ah, go on home you Pitjentjarra rubbish.

Go home yourself you Aranda babies.

That's the way it goes, Mister. Every time we have a mock spear battle we finish up wishing we had shovel-nosed hunting spears.

Do you wonder that the tribes once engaged in mortal wars which would have made the Knights of Old blanch with fear?

Hundreds of men would line up on the plains and throw spears at each other until they ran out of ammunition. Then they'd throw the enemy's spears back at him — and warriors were often killed with their own weapons.

Nevertheless, some of the tribes have adopted Rules of War which the United Nations might examine. Take the Gobaboingu, for instance, at Millingimbi on the Arnhem Land coast.

249

When they have a fight or someone has a grievance a peace-making ceremony called Magarada is held.

An aggrieved person is given a number of 'free shots' with spears at the offender. He makes a great display of wrath but actually throws to miss — there is really big trouble if his 'miss' is off-line and kills the poor fellow.

After a few such shots the offender presents his thigh to the aggrieved who nicks it with a spear point or a knife and draws blood. Honour is thus satisfied. At night the entire tribe turns up for a full-dress corroboree at which fresh grievances begin, requiring another peace-making ceremony and a further corroboree.

That's where we get the phrase 'Ad Magaradum', which means 'You do it to me and I'll do it to you.'

Among some of the Roper River tribes peace-making fights known as Banburr are conducted with shin-cracking nulla-nullas made of ironwood. Ironwood is as heavy and as hard as it sounds.

Banburr is a ceremonial corroboree in which grudges are settled in free-for-all fights of extreme violence. The combatants belabour each other unmercifully until blood runs in rivulets, bones are broken and heads are cracked. But aboriginal heads are so tough that often a nulla-nulla cracks first.

The corroboree may go on for two or three days, crowded by men and women who come from afar to watch and participate as they might have done at a Roman Tournament.

The Banburr ground is a bedlam of hysterical noise: the screams of pain, the dull thud of waddies, the fearful crack of bones being broken.

Women take part, too, jabbing and cutting each other with yam sticks for alleged pilfering of husbands and other indiscretions. They are worse than the men, fighting with intense malice, yelling imprecations, and simmering long after the men have quietened down.

But quieten they must, for Banburr is the Peace Table, the battle-ground where staggering warriors sign an armistice in blood. The price of a man's pardon is high. It might be fingers or an arm shattered by a hammer-blow from a nulla-nulla; it might be an eye dug out with a yam stick. Yet when it is finished all grudges truly cease to exist. The combatants sit down together and exchange presents.

However, to get back to these Pitjentjarra rubbish: We beat 'em, didn't we, Mister? They're really a bunch of scaredy-cats.

Oh, yes, I'll admit we ran behind that big boulder a few times but so would you if you had a spear coming at you at fifty miles an hour.

By the way, did you hear about Billy Larrakia, the Tiwi tribesman who was said to be the champion spear-thrower in the Northern Territory?

He was so good that they began training him on the javelin for the Olympic Games. I mean, a man who had hunted and fought with spears all his life should have been hot stuff with a javelin.

Billy was flown down to Sydney for a sports meeting and put on a mighty show. He huffed and he puffed and he threw it about 150 feet.

The first white man to compete against him threw it 250 feet.

And in the Olympic Games the record was established at 280 feet.

Since then Billy hasn't taken much interest in spear-throwing. He gets all his meals out of a tin.

And he talks all the time about importing a few white javelin throwers as professional hunters.

Desert Boys

PINTUBI TRIBE

CENTRAL AUSTRALIA

←————————————————————————————

HEY, KIDS, LOOK AT this guy with the white skin and the furry stuff all over him. Hey Mister, what d'ya call that stuff?

Do you mean his clothes?

Clothes? Never heard of them. What are they for?

To hide his skin.

Why does he want to hide his skin?

So other people won't see it and to keep him warm.

They must be queer people these white fellers. Hey Mister, what's that thing he's got in his ears?

You know nothing, you Myall boy. That's a stethoscope. The man's a doctor. With it he can listen to you inside your skin.

Can't he hear me if I sing out?

Yes, yes, but this is different-kind.

I haven't got a voice inside.

The doctor is listening to your heart and your chest.

What's heart? What's chest?

Oh shut up you Myall boy. You know what chest and heart are.

Fair dinkum, Mister, we never heard of them.

Well, they are part of your body.

Like foot and hand?

Yes, like foot and hand, but inside your skin.

My father says only spirit inside my skin.

Well, your father is a Myall, too.

253

Hey, Mister, what's that thing on his wrist.
That's a watch, you Myall boy.
Watch? What's a watch for, Mister?
That's to tell the time. Watch says when it's time to get up, tucker time, work time, sleep time.

But I know all that and I haven't got a watch. The sun tells me when to get up. My belly tells me when to eat. I don't know about work — my people have never tried it. At sundown I know it's bed time.

> White man properly different kind,
> Watch on wrist, then wind . . . wind . . . wind;
> Pull up sleeve and look all day,
> Look when work and look when play.

> Man look time then say 'Must go'.
> Man look clock and then him know
> Time is Boss; all understand
> Must keep eye on face and hand.

> 'Tick . . . tock . . . tock,' that wrist-watch say,
> 'Me big Boss, you do my way,
> 'I make you wait and I make you run,
> 'I make you work when you like fun.

> 'I send off coach . . . I send off train,
> 'My hand start big aeroplane;
> 'Big-feller Boss, he must watch me,
> 'Breakfast, dinner, supper and tea.'

> My man listen and then him say,
> 'No time sleep and no time stay,
> 'Too much hurry down the street,
> 'Awful time when no time eat'.

Hey, Mister, what's that funny box with the glass eye?
That's a camera, you Myall boy.

254

Camera? What's a camera?

It takes your photograph when I press this button.

Photograph? What's a photograph, Mister?

It's an image of you, like you see in a mirror.

Mirror? What's a mirror, Mister?

Well . . . it's a piece of glass.

Glass? What's glass, Mister?

Good heavens! Are you all Myalls out here? Haven't you seen a white man before? Or any of his everyday goods?

No, Mister, you are the first white man we have seen. Until today none of us had seen clothes or watches or cameras or mirrors or glass. Hey, Mister, what about some more of that scrummy tinned tucker? It's better than rats and lizards.

You mean you eat rats and lizards?

Sure, Mister. Doesn't everyone?

Certainly not. How revolting!

Hey, kids, look at this Myall with the camera. He doesn't like rats and lizards.

(Author's Note: Dr. John Hargrave, shown here, was a member of the first government patrol to make contact with the Pintubi tribe near the border of Western Australia and the Northern Territory. This photo was taken by the leader of the patrol, Mr. E. C. Evans. Myall: A woolly primitive.)

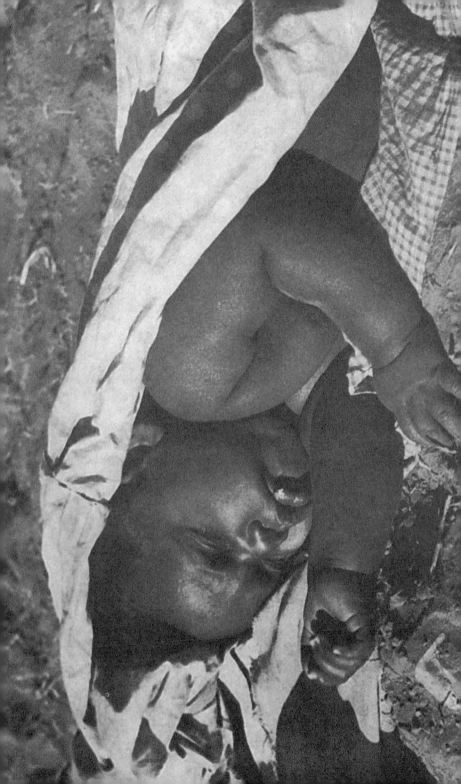

The New Generation

MALAK MALAK TRIBE

DALY RIVER, NORTH AUSTRALIA

WELL, THAT'S THE STORY.

Here I am with the world at my feet, a brand new member of the rising generation.

I can go the way of my ancestors and become a primitive hunter on the vast plains of the Moil and Daly Rivers between Darwin and Port Keats or, like old Barney Barrgirr, live on the fish I would catch in the streams.

Alternatively, I can take over from Charcoal and Midnight as students in the mission school where I will learn to read and write and become a sophisticated black man.

Perhaps I will take the education that is now being so freely offered.

My people have been illiterate stockmen for too long.

It is time we broke away from this old tradition.

I may become a teacher myself, passing on book learning instead of tribal mysteries, miracles and witchcraft.

For me the future is secure. I lie asleep in the sand on the bank of the Daly River with a full belly, content in the knowledge that there is plenty more where this lot came from.

Unless I choose, I will never be forced to hunt for my food as my ancestors were.

In the years to come my mother and father will tell me about the droughts, the famine and the starvation of hundreds of our people who live on the inland plains not so many miles south of here.

For them, too, the end of want has come.

The terrible story of our decimation is being reversed. After two hundred years of increasing death we have arrested our tribal decline and regained the will to live.

No longer do the squatters chant:

> 'They shall grow not old as we who are white grow old.
> 'Age shall not weary them nor the years condemn;
> 'At the going down of the sun, and in the morning
> 'We will dismember them.'

We do not have to worry about being shot down like kangaroos.

We are no longer legally chained by policemen as in the old days, whether we were murderers or witnesses to murder.

It is many years since any native has had his head pulled off by a rope, whether on a scaffold or a tree or while being dragged behind a vehicle.

The restraining jackets and the ringbolts have disappeared from the prisons.

People still call us 'Niggers', 'Damned niggers', and 'Bloody useless niggers'.

We don't mind the swearing, which is normal in an average Aussie's vocabulary.

But easy on the 'Niggers', sport. That is part of the racial prejudice which a learned old white gentleman once described as 'the vilest manifestation of a diseased mind.'

Well, I'll be seeing you.

Watch for me and my brothers in the halls of fame.

If I could be granted just one wish, it would be that a poem called 'Two-Feller Level 'Gether', written by our old mate Bill Harney, should become part of the curriculum in all white schools:

> Missus' boy and my little boy two-feller grow up 'gether,
> Level play in mud all day longa the rainy weather;

Two-feller chase'im dog all-time, fight and climb'im tree,
Listen hard when my man tell stories longa to we.

That little white kid like'im me, properly nice-one boy,
My old man go bush all day, cut'im out boomerang toy;
Two-feller play-play all the day, one feller black one white,
Two-feller same when play at game, two-feller level fight.

And my old man 'im say to me, 'must be someone mad:
'White-feller think him all-time good, blackfeller all time bad.'
But kiddie 'im no-more think that way, two-feller level play,
White-feller talk-talk one-feller God, two-feller level pray.

Blackfeller all day help'im white, somebody must be fool,
Whitefeller boy go different kind whenever 'im go to school.
'Can't understand,' my old man say, 'somewhere somebody mad.'
But I no-more listen, me only see two kid happy and glad.

So I talk, 'Old man, listen here, no more growl-growl white,
'All-about must live 'im way, which one say 'im right?
'Kiddie 'im play-play every day, kiddie 'im no-more fool,
'Two-feller level understand when two-feller level school.'

THE END